The Sacred

of

The Desert

African Philosophical Transcendence

By Mocholoko, Zulumathabo Zulu

Foreword by Professor Connie Zulu of North West University, South Africa

First Edition
1.0

Mocholoko, Zulumathabo Zulu: *Lexicographer, Doctoral Practitioner, Software Engineer, Indigenous Knowledge Expert, Metaphysical Scientist, Cosmologist, Inventor and Research Analyst.*

Madisebo University College Press

Published By:
*Madisebo University College Press

First Published in South Africa 2014. First Published in America 2019.
Publication © Madisebo University College Press 2019
Text © Zulumathabo Zulu 2019
Photos © Zulumathabo Zulu 2019
Artwork © Zulumathabo Zulu 2019

Inquiries should be addressed to:

Email: zulumathabo@yahoo.ca

Blog: www.zulumathabo.com

ISBN: 978-0-620-59937-5

Printed in United States of America

Dedication

A well-deserved tribute to the great Nubia; the descendant daughter of the venerable Nama people of Keetmanshoop in the land of the brave Namibia. It is my endless hope that you were able to survive the extremes of the Kalahari Desert and the jungle of Dukwe where the apartheid forces worked very hard for our demise.

This book is dedicated to the traditional surgeon and the great *Ngaka* Madisebo Moloi. May her sacred heart, beautiful spirit and vibrations of the galactic core persist as guiding lights of genesis to inspire selfless service, unconditional love and truth seeking as we continue to advance the fulfillment of her aweinspiring deeds long after her departure.

Acknowledgments

This book is inspired by the literary piece *Venturesome Kisses* in the books <u>A Goodbye To My Little Troubles</u> and <u>A Woman In The Bush</u>.

I am forever indebted to Abram Mlangeni, *Ngaka* Madisebo and *Nyanga* Masangane for all the indigenous knowledge they passed on to me. The philosophical constructs in this book are inspired by the venerated ancestors of the Matamong village.

Thank you to Dr. Gina Vale of Toronto, Canada for her reading, proofreading and suggested improvements of The Philosophy chapter. Dr. Vale is a member of the Italian Writers Association of Toronto which warmly welcomed me as part of their community while I lived in Toronto thanks to Bruna Di Giuseppe-Bertoni and Michael Mirolla. The Italian community of Toronto shall forever be cherished by me for all their love, warmth and open mind while I was exiled from my homeland of South Africa an experience that I regard as a credit to humanity. Those barbecue book readings held at your homes continue to echo like distant Tibetan singing bowls during the invocation of my memory of the great land of Canada.

A special thank you to the Chairman of South Africa's Freedom Park Council, Mr. Vusi Mchunu who read and provided a positive feedback about <u>The Sacred Knowledge of the Desert</u>. Macingwane! Ndima! Majola! Mbense! Nyanda! Ngqulunga!

Mr. Mchunu shared his impressions of this book as shown below:

The metaphor of the "desert flower" instantly invokes resilience, resistance, camouflage, existence, the environment and the alignment with time and the cosmos. Professor Lesiba Joseph Teffo of the University of South Africa's School of Transdisciplinary Research Institutes expresses a more succinct and relevant definition, *"The Ecosystem perspective, closely related to the interdisciplinary approach, allows us to view phenomena, institutions and practices as an ecosystem that evolves within an environment defined by social, cultural, political and economic conditions to produce particular performance outcomes."*

Zulu's rare combination of verse and prose style is akin to the eclectic tongues of great classics like <u>Black Skin, White Masks</u> by Frantz Fanon and <u>Two Thousand Seasons</u> by Ayi Kwei Armah, written in allegorical tone and shifting from autobiographical and realistic details to philosophical pondering, effectively prophesying a new age. Zulu's pre-occupation with re-discovering African Indigenous Knowledge Systems, integrating Western science with African science, haranguing the wretched amongst the African descendants never to give up, is a loud and clarion call. Zulumathabo is charting a path deserving of a better acclaim and tumultuous celebration.

The Sacred Knowledge of the Desert by Zulumathabo Zulu is a daring exercise in thought provocation and motivation coming to us in a form of a book that teaches the vital lessons of life. Using a rare combination of analytical prose and contextual verse as a medium of delivery, Zulumathabo or the 'shepherd boy' as he always calls himself, foregrounds the ideal human experience with respect to handling and managing the adverse challenges of life.

The ideal experience is that a human must be able to transcend adversity instead of being defined by it regardless of the intensity of a particular version of adversity. He uses the imagery of the desert flower to depict the potential ability inherent in all of us to transcend adversity despite the contraption of adversity or our different walks of life.

Instead of being proscribed and defined by harsh conditions as is the case when a human is ordinarily befallen by hard times, the desert flower transmutes the raw energy of adversity into good energy in order to inspire the beautiful geometry and brilliant colours of its petals so that it appears as if "*There was no problem*" as expressed in a contextual poem The Desert Corolla.

More poetry from the literary piece unfolds as follows:

Despite a low rainfall
Despite a dehydrated ground
Despite sun rays that kill
She rises from the waterless
Unimpeded by soil eroded
The brilliant petals uncorroded

This journey of life, to some extent reminiscent of his own life, has led the author to be inspired by the desert which he sees as a place of tranquility, sanctuary and instructive schooling in terms of drawing energy from adversity instead of losing energy to it. This is because the author sees the desert not as a wasteland but rather as a place of sacred beauty.

From humble beginnings as a shepherd boy in the Free State province of South Africa, Zulumathabo has transcended adversity, destitution and exile in many countries to emerge as a mature intellectual and philosopher who firmly embraces indigenous knowledge and ways of knowing. The desert flower is our indigenous school of life from which we can learn what it means to produce beauty despite bleak conditions as is the case when a desert flower produces a breathtaking corolla in a dehydrated ground as expressed in The Desert Corolla.

For the author of this book, the desert holds sacred knowledge and optimism which the only one with a black belt in transcending existential complexity can unravel and portray. This book demonstrates in a powerful way the value of feistiness, resilience and optimism in spite of life's struggles.

The sharp contrast of the desert as a symbol of desolation and barrenness, and the desert flower as a symbol of vitality, hope and survival represents a promise of fertility, life, progress and emancipation. For this reason, the desert flower effectively transforms the desert into a place of serene beauty and transcendence.

The analogy of the desert and the flower can apply to any human circumstance where the human spirit needs to triumph over some form of adversity. Readers from any walks of life can relate to the message in this book that success and victory are possible no matter what obstacles life throws at you. It is possible to achieve one's dreams and goals with self-discipline and restraint. Forging ahead and taking risks in life are necessary preconditions for emancipation, freedom and eventual success.

The Sacred Knowledge of the Desert is a profound lesson of hope. This is a book that speaks and uplifts everybody. It transcends socio-cultural, socio-economic and philosophical orientations. Its central image – the desert flower – is at once aweinspiring and deeply spiritual in the simplicity of its message which is to inspire hope in the face of things falling apart.

This compelling and truly motivating message is firmly grounded in the pragmatic experience of the desert flower. The message of hope that permeates this book has universal appeal that resonates with all human beings regardless of their unique situation. The reading of this book is a lesson in optimism, resilience and tenacity.

We can all take a 'leaf' from this book and draw strength and comfort in the knowledge that no matter how bleak our prevailing circumstances, there is always a light at the end of the tunnel, and like the desert flower, the sun will always 'smile' upon us and the rain will fall and revive us and cause us to blossom and radiate life and vitality as expressed in another literary piece Venturesome Kisses, as follows:

Forbidden grounds of love cast their spell. The naivety of love sweetens the love that exists like a desert flower. Deprived of water, the flower waits underground until, when the rains fall, it springs to life, knowing that the rain will soon be gone.

The 'shepherd boy' has come full circle and so have I. The Sacred Knowledge of the Desert evokes nostalgia in accordance with the awesome beauty of two very different natural phenomena as was the Atlantic Ocean on the one hand and the Namib desert on the other which arrested my attention while visiting Namibia. I was spellbound by the natural beauty of the Namib desert. The ocean and the desert side by side was breathtaking to behold and each had its unique therapeutic effect. The sharp contrast was out of this world, as was the sobering thought of the struggle for survival that occurs for the permanent inhabitants of these places.

In conclusion, we draw from the contextual commentary of the Desert Corolla as follows:

Eventually, the great desert flower delivered some aweinspiring corolla with bright petals dancing in the wind and never to be overruled by adversity.

Professor Connie Zulu, DEd
Research Niche Area Coordinator and Lecturer – Educational Management, North-West University, South Africa

A desert plant must solve the survival problem that arises as a result of the environmental stresses associated with trying to make a living in the desert. The gyrations of being subjected to extreme heat, extreme drought, extreme cold nights or some extreme event must be correctly managed in order to mitigate the damage to the organism. Unlike an animal organism that can choose to run away from a situation that poses a dangerous threat to its survival, the plant organism is inescapably bound to that situation and running away is not a viable option.

For this reason, the audacious plant has to be resourceful enough to come up with ingenious ways to solve the pressing problem that threatens its survival or else the plant faces a cruel choice of adapt or die. Even though the desert is a harsh place, there is a lot of wisdom in the desert. The Sacred Knowledge of the Desert is intended to uncover this wisdom and harness it in order to become wiser from it. The desert plant has learnt to harness this wisdom overtime and it will show us how we can tap into this rich source of wisdom. This desert wisdom is part of the DNA of the desert plant.

One of the most powerful concepts of this desert knowledge is that it is possible for an organism to transcend adversity so that it is not bracketed by it. This means adversity is one of the normal occurrences in life but without its arresting powers. The fetters of adversity are apparently invisible to the organism. Though subdued, the organism is apparently not able to see the fetters being subdued. The organism must tackle the arresting fetters of adversity in real-time to avoid being shackled by them.

How does the organism tackle the invisible fetters[1]? How does the organism restrain what it cannot visualize? If the organism can tackle and hold down the fetters, it will gain a new experience of transcendence over adversity. It's the ability to restrain the fetters of adversity that will enable the organism to transcend the harsh conditions and set it apart from others.

Moreover, the ability to transcend adversity requires a helicopter view of the situation. Through the helicopter view of the topography, the organism sees all kinds of things like the sand dunes, the beautiful colour of the desert, the beautiful geometry of the desert, the desert plants, the horizon where heaven and earth meet, the people who live in the desert and the oasis that sustains them.

Interestingly, the desert has lots of merciful kindness despite being an inhospitable place. This merciful kindness allows the residents who have chosen

---

[1] The apparent fetters of adversity may also come in a form of a spell in the experience of the organism making it hard for the organism to shake off this spell.

to live here to continue to be. The desert plant, like other residents of the desert, is a recipient of this merciful kindness. When the going gets tough in the desert, the flower uses biochemistry, transcendence and the glorious appearing in order to outshine the darkness of adversity and thrive.

The Biochemistry of Adaptation

Different plants have different strategies but they all synthesize HSPs (heat shock proteins) to cope with heat shock and the ABAs (abscisic acids) to cope with water deprivation. It's the HSP strategy that gives the desert plant an ability to tolerate heat shock whereas the ABA hormonal strategy gives the plant the ability to tolerate water shortage and thus protect itself from dehydration.

A human mind gets fixated on a tough situation very easily. He becomes demotivated very easily. He loses interest in things that used to excite him when he gets depressed or becomes anxious. He self-destructs if he is blocked from forging ahead. The self-destructing ways also mean he poses a danger to others around him unless a solution is found that emancipates him from his destructive ways.

Sometimes organizational procedures make him feel like a trapped animal that has been cornered and is unable to exit the stifling corner. He can particularly become a danger to those close to him like his colleagues, family or friends. All these experiences can become an explosive mix that leads a human on a destructive path if he feels he has run out of options. It is the critical mission of this book to equip a human with intellectual fighting sticks to assist him in getting out of a dark corner.

Transcendence

Every organism has a share of adversity in its life in one form or another but to be defined and limited by this adverse experience is not the way to be. Considering that adversity is not a new thing, it must be possible for an organism to develop adaptive skills and the behaviour patterns that allow it to rise above adverse conditions. Transcending adversity would be the single most important skill for an organism.

In transcending adversity, what are we transcending? Are we transcending adversity itself or the experience of adversity? Or are we transcending the perceptions of adversity? Which one is it?

We experience the environment through our sensory systems. If the environment is cold then our skin sensory system reports the cold experience via the afferent pathways to our brain. If there is a threatening stimulus like crossing a crocodile-infested river, then our visual system reports the visual stimulus via the ganglion cells to our brain. If there is a sound of a snake, our acoustic processing system reports to our brain the acoustic stimulus.

All the various sensory systems create the experience of the environment. The experience and the processing of it determines the quality of knowledge that can come out of it. The environment may give us an empirical or perceptual knowledge based on the type of experience we have. For this reason, there are two types of experience namely (1) empirical experience and (2) perceptual experience.

Empirical Experience

This experience is reporting to us the state of the environment whether our survival is threatened or enhanced. We don't want to alter or temper with this kind of experience. It must always report the truth to us. We must maintain the fidelity to the state of the environment.

The Perceptual Experience

This is the secondary type of experience that comes to us after registering the empirical impressions of the object or phenomenon in our brain. This kind of experience is a subjective analysis of the environment which is greatly influenced by our past experience and knowledge of the environment. It is the perceptual experience that we must transcend. If the perceptual experience is propagating a cold experience, we can propagate a warm experience via the efferent system.

In order to propagate a positive experience in the midst of adversity, the organism must be pro-active. When jabbed repeatedly by adversity without some adaptive response to the situation, the organism becomes anxious and transfixed by the adverse experience as if frozen in its tracks like a mouse in the presence of a snake. This only serves to disempower the organism making the organism feel like a beginner in spite of having experienced the same situation many times before.

Something is short circuiting the brain of the organism so that it is unable to learn from the experience. What is missing here is some kind of productive action on the part of the organism. The Sesotho axiom "Haetheteha e ya ntlafala" is in order here. This axiom says "When it rolls, it gets renewed".

The propositional statement is instructing the organism to shake off the inertia. The organism must get rolling. Instead of being anxious, transfixed or mesmerized by the novel situation, the organism must do something useful like launching some counterstrike, making some noise or walking away from the situation and never to be defined by it. Adversity needs to know that for every action there is an equal and timely reaction. In this way, adversity will retreat and think twice before casting a witchy spell upon the organism. Hereafter, the organism will gain traction towards transcendence over adversity.

The great desert flower Mponeng has this unique skill of transcending adversity so that she is not defined by it. Instead, Mponeng defines and configures adversity according to her own style. This approach makes her the master of her own destiny. Shouldn't you as a human being be a master of your own destiny?

A Glorious Appearing

A desert plant like Mponeng is always looking forward to the glorious appearing of the falling rain. The great hope of the glorious appearing is such a vitalizing sensation that it recharges the internal batteries of the desert plant. The desert flower even gyrates underground listening to the slightest indications of the falling rain as reported (poetry section of this book) in the contextual commentary of Unconquerable Like a Desert Flower as follows:

"The unconquerable desert flower Mponeng of the great Kalahari remains watchful underground listening to the slightest indications of the falling rain."

It's like the plant is sniffing for this distant rain. The dark clouds that hang over the desert from the sky or the dark clouds of dust storms that arise from the ground do not conceal the imminence of this coming rain. When the rains fall, Mponeng springs to life like a coiled Masumu of Matamong knowing that the rain is not here forever and may soon be the thing of the past as reported in Venturesome Kisses.

The desert flower wants to make sure that she absorbs the rain as much as possible to an extent of storing more rain in her succulents so that when the rain is gone, she can continue to dance in the breeze while living off the reserves of the rain that fell. The desert flower can do this because she has learnt not only to enjoy the rain but also to internalize the rain as reported in the contextual commentary of Part of the DNA. Thus, the desert flower is greatly inspired by the coming of the falling rain.

Finally, this book is intended to demonstrate how a desert flower transcends adversity, how a desert flower is a powerful model in our lives and how this model can energize a human spirit despite adversity having this power to exact stringent punishment upon those thus visited. Accordingly, we want to motivate the sons and daughters of the African soil and the Diaspora and wherever they may be such as in the corporations, companies, organizations, government agencies, institutions, communities or homes.

Table of Contents

Enter the desert flower. These are the transcendental teachings of the desert flower whose visionary mission is to meet the falling rain, dance in the breeze, wear the greenest leaves and be the most beautiful flower in the desert while passing on the best survival and cultural knowledge to the next generation. Despite the constant water shortage and the dehydrated ground of the harsh desert, her unshaken belief in the coming rain is the mother of all belief systems designed to outshine any darkness cast on her path.

She brings to us very simple teachings such as the indefatigable vision that enables transcendence over adversity, the survival template of the surround which ensures a well-directed and resourced behaviour and the problem solving ability that inspires creative thinking, tenacity and fortitude.

Why The Desert Flower?

There are many schools of thought in which the teaching of wisdom could have come to us. People learn wisdom from the grade school, the FET[2] school, the university school or the church school. Nonetheless, we are going to learn wisdom from a different school.

We are proposing a paradigm shift in terms of teaching wisdom. Our school is the desert. We are going to learn wisdom from the desert school. The professor of the desert school is the great desert flower Mponeng. The desert flower Mponeng is a legend and a pedagogue. She is also a wisdom keeper extraordinaire making her a legend.

We have been socialized into a variety of traditional systems of learning that use words to teach a new concept. They use words to teach you how to behave in a particular way. They use words to teach you how to count. They use words to teach you how to play a particular game or sport. Words are used as a platform of passing knowledge to others.

Unlike the learning systems that use words to teach, the desert uses examples, objects and modeling to teach wisdom. The desert school uses participatory observation as a way of teaching wisdom. This means the teaching objective is to modify and enhance the student by means of this amazing wisdom that comes to us through observation, modeling and storytelling hereafter referred to as OMS. This is because OMS concepts are anchored in reality. You can only observe reality. You can only model reality. Storytelling coming out of observation and

---

[2] South Africa's tertiary education system known as Further Education and Training. This is similar to North America's concept of community colleges.

modeling can only be based on reality. This kind of OMS teaching is a paradigm shift from the normal words-based teaching in which we get harangued about this and that.

In the desert school there are fewer words but more examples of wisdom as a modality of teaching. For example, if we want to learn the principle of transcending adversity, we just have to observe how the desert flower transcends and solves the puzzling adversity of water shortage. If we want to learn the principle of positive thinking and living, we just have to observe how the desert flower shows off its beautiful petals out of a dehydrated ground. If we want to learn the principle of overcoming divisions in our midst, we just have to observe how the desert flower produces buds and some nice green out of the cracks of the dehydrated ground. After observing the above principles, we use modeling to simulate how these principles apply to our lives and our problem solving projects. There is no better teacher than the desert flower and it is the mission of this book to teach you the wisdom of the desert from The Sacred Knowledge of the Desert school.

Why Is This Important?

The desert flower is the greatest gift to humanity in terms of understanding our life's purpose and finding sustainable ways to fulfill that purpose. Our purpose in life is a strategic mission that must transcend everything else after fulfilling our basic needs of survival.

Using words to teach a concept is something that belongs to the domain of traditional schools like the grade school, the FET school, the University school and the church school as previously mentioned

The problem with words is that they are not anchored in reality. Words are based on thought patterns of the mind and how it finds it convenient to express those thought patterns. Words tend to shift the goal posts in order to make a certain point. The truth can be expressed or suppressed using words. Words can be used to describe reality and can also be used to alter reality. This is the case when words are used to assert that God exists like the believer, that God does not exist like the atheist or that we cannot be sure of the existence or non-existence of God like the agnostic. In the foregoing example, one can neither prove nor disprove the truth of the phenomenon.

The problem of words is endemic to other knowledge domains like the scientific establishment which asserts that a Sangoma refers to things that are not observable and therefore cannot be vouched for using the scientific method. However, the interesting fact is that the scientific establishment uses a microscope to convince us about the unobservable phenomena which cannot be independently observed. Scientific words are then used to rationally persuade our belief in the phenomenon that is not independently observable.

Let's take an example of a tree. If I say this is a tree, you will also agree that this is a tree because you can independently observe the tree. You don't have to rely on my assertion that the tree exists. The existence of the tree does not need words to convince us of its existence. Thus, the tree commands an objective existence and our belief cannot materially alter the existence of the tree.

This tree phenomenon is independently observable but that is not the case with a microscope phenomenon where we only have to rely on the microscope and the scientist telling us about the phenomenon which we are not able to independently observe. How is that different from the Sangoma who is reporting about an unobservable phenomenon?

Note that the lack of independent observation is not a reflection on the truth or lack thereof with respect to the unobservable phenomenon. The interested reader is referred to another book The Sangoma and the Microscope by this author for a detailed analytical discussion of the subject.

The desert school avoids the problem of words by rather focusing on the objects of reality and the modeling of reality in its natural environment. The desert flower does not use words to teach or convince us about a particular concept or behaviour. It demonstrates to us through its life how it interacts with natural challenges that are thrown in its path.

The desert flower teaches us how it transcends the constraints of the environment through its actions and ways of thinking. In this way, we can learn to transcend the constraints imposed by adversity by emulating the behaviour of the desert flower.

This paradigm shift in the art and science of didactics also means we have to unlearn certain things. We have to unlearn the use of words as the only way of teaching and learning a new concept. We are now forced to find inventive ways of teaching and learning a concept using observational skills, modeling skills and storytelling skills. This is a humble way of conducting a teaching and learning situation. This is also a humble way of participating in a teaching and learning situation.

The desert flower is continuously battered and tossed back and forth by the shortage of water, the dust particles, the lashing winds, the killer sun rays and the stringent consequences associated with trying to make a living in an inhospitable place like the desert. Nonetheless, the desert flower is graciously cognizant of the most important thing in her life which is the falling rain. The desert flower does not compromise this sacred purpose regardless of the excessive amount of adversity that she has to contend with in the vast and undulating desert.

The desert flower maintains the clarity of her vision and composure of her survival behaviour at all times. It would be impossible to survive the extreme conditions of the desert without a guiding vision.

This kind of visionary approach provides a helicopter view with respect to the terrain in which Mponeng finds herself. It enables her to appreciate the most important things and how they relate to her life's purpose. The harsh vagaries of existence like the dust particles, the sand, the parched ground and the lack of water do not get in the way of that vision.

The desert flower has mastered this kind of transcendence over the adversity that emanates from the dehydrated ground. She is born into a parched ground. She grows up in a parched ground that sometimes manifests itself through gaping cracks. She is born into the adversity of the unforgiving desert and yet she is not defined by that adversity. The desert flower is almost like a fish that is born in an extremely salty environment and yet it must be salted before it can be eaten.

After being tested in the dehydrating desert, the desert flower has become purified like a polished diamond in the fire of harsh conditions. Subsequent to the rainfall, she exhibits flawless colours as if she was not singed off in the fiery desert. She shows off some nice green as if she never suffered from the harsh conditions of water shortage. She dances in the breeze as if the planet is a playground and not a dangerous place. She is the first to welcome the coming rain as if she enjoys a preferential treatment from the heavens. This is the kind of attitude humans must espouse and exhibit in order to fulfill their purpose on this planet by transcending the mould of adversity that they are cast into.

For this reason, the desert flower is the greatest gift to all humanity regardless of status or station in life. Perhaps you are a university or college professor reading this book. Perhaps you are a school teacher reading this book. Perhaps you are student reading this book. Perhaps you are a community member reading this book. Perhaps you are a company employee reading this book. Perhaps you are a corporate executive reading this book. Whatever the case may be, this book is intended to effect a powerful transformative experience in your personal and organizational life for the better.

From a philosophical and truth-seeking point of view, the desert flower Mponeng is committed to the idea of wanting to transcend, outdo, overtake or outshine adversity no matter what. The desert flower wants to come out with the upper hand despite the things that suck her energy and frustrate her path. She trusts her instincts and follows her intuition when sorting through a list of challenges that awaits her.

Through the pages of this book and in accordance with the indefatigable spirit of the great desert flower Mponeng, you are going to become vibrant, renewed, revitalized and ready to fulfill your purpose. Come with me as I show the way. I am the work of art that has been chiseled, shaped, polished and enhanced by adversity and I shall always draw electric power from the eternal teachings of the unfaltering desert flower; an amazing life form that inspires us all without failing.

Section One: The Philosophy

The African ancients define the concept of transcendence as mean "undefined" which advances a contrarian view of transcendence vis-à-vis the way transcendence is commonly understood and used by ordinary people. This section, on philosophical transcendence, provides a gentle introduction to the cosmic origins of African philosophy as discovered via in-depth investigation of the philosophical constructs of the Basotho people of South Africa in the Free State province.

The African desert philosophy necessitates that we espouse the originality of thought so that we are in a position to contribute novel ideas to the subject and come away better educated than before. Moreover, Southern Africa is a region whose indigenous history was subjected to an abrupt interruption by colonization with the result that the indigenous philosophy of the African natives is not known. This led to the authentic African way of scholarly tradition becoming frozen in time while the new antithesis of Eurocentricity displaced the original thesis of Afrocentricity in the land of the ancestors. This book chapter offers an excellent opportunity to revive and present an indigenous African philosophy.

The Setting

The setting of this book is located in the desert of Kalahari. The desert basin of Kalahari is found in most countries of Southern Africa including South Africa, Botswana, Angola, Zambia, Zimbabwe and Namibia. The word Kalahari comes from the Setswana name Kgalakgadi which refers to the desert. Kgalakgadi means the place of great water shortage. For many of us, the desert is a source of our teachings, inspiration and energy.

Although set in the Kgalakgadi, the book draws from other African deserts like the Namib Desert. When the author visited the Namib[3] Desert at Swakopmund and Walvis Bay, he was awe-struck by the juxtaposition of the desert on the one hand and the Atlantic Ocean on the other. There is nothing like this that the author has ever seen in many countries he traveled. This also evoked the nostalgia of the great country of Canada. The author felt that if he sailed North West along the Atlantic, he would eventually arrive in Eastern Canada, where he spent most of his life in Ottawa.

---

[3] The author expresses gratitude to Dr. Kagiso Moloi and his family of Namibia for making it possible for the author to visit Namibia and experience the Namib Desert. Makgolokwe a matle! Makotswana! Dikgomo tseo le manamane a tsona. The former Councilor Klassen of Namibian Parliament who traveled with us and provided narrative accounts of the desert, the people of the desert and the Atlantic Ocean is remembered. Also with us was Norberth the son of the Herero Paramount Chief Vekui Rukoro.

Introduction

This chapter provides the genesis, the cosmic knowledge of Dumelang[4], the triangle knowledge system and the philosophical principles needed to gain transcendence over adverse conditions in which organisms find themselves. We begin with the genesis.

The Genesis

The Basotho, like other Africans, trace their genesis to the cosmos. They originate from Mokgubu wa Kganare (*The Galactic Core*). One of their most valued stars is Tosamasiu (Sirius) which is regarded as a ternary star system. They refer to the orbiting star of Tosamasiu known as Peo Ya Makgakga (*The Seed of Makgakga*). Makgakga is not visible to the naked eye. Another star Mabeleha (*A fertile woman sorghum*) is not visible to a naked eye.

As if that is not incredible enough, Basotho also pay tribute to Tosa (Jupiter). Their astronomical axiom says "Hobona tosa le madinyana a yona" meaning "To see Jupiter along with its youngs". The youngs refer to the moons of Jupiter. These moons are not visible to the naked eye.

How could they have known about the orbiting stars of Tosamasiu without being assisted by some instrument? How could they have known of the invisible moons of Jupiter? Without a technological instrument of any kind, the Basotho know about invisible stellar bodies. This is yet another confirmation that they are indeed from the cosmos. They don't need telescopes to trace their origins to the cosmos. This astronomical knowledge was passed on to them by their foremothers and forefathers across many generations, and long before the advent of the Europeans in South Africa.

Recently, while I was awake and reflecting on Tosamasiu, Peo Ya Makgakga and Mabeleha, I was visited by a voice of a female messenger from this star system of Tosamasiu. Thokoza Makhosi! The last time I heard a voice like this was more than 30 years ago at the village of Mmakwane as recorded in the books <u>A Goodbye To My Little Troubles</u> and <u>A Woman in the Bush</u>. At that time, I was walking under the willow trees in the former homeland of QwaQwa when I heard the voice instructing me to take a different path upon my return. I complied with this voice and consequently became imbued with the ancestral spirit of Mmakwane.

This time around, I was at Mafikeng and it was in the morning when the voice said the messenger had arrived. I was awake as was the case with the voice of

---

[4] Basotho greeting.

Mmakwane. This was a voice of a very young woman. This messenger was from the distant star system of Tosamasiu. Thokoza Makhosi! I was greatly humbled, enlightened and energized by this voice of the heavens. This is yet another spiritual manifestation of the messengers of the cosmos.

Since the Africans trace their genesis to the cosmos, the cosmos has shaped their way of life. The star system of Tosamasiu is connected to Mabele (sorghum); a very important crop among the Africans. In addition to being a source of food for humans and a sacred food of the gods, Mabele is also a form of nutritional medicine. With high amounts of potassium and fibre, people who eat Mabele in the countryside do not suffer from metabolic illnesses like diabetes, high blood pressure, stomach or rectal cancer as is the case with those who dwell in urban centres. When they need to communicate with the spirits, the African natives offer Mabele to the ancestors.

This cosmic knowledge has also shaped the African philosophy of science with respect to matter. The way we know and understand matter is that it is a material that occupies space and has mass. Matter consists of an atom. When you further break down an atom, you find that it consists of electrons, protons and neutrons. An atom is a particle. The electrons, protons and neutrons are also particles. Thus, according to a Western theory of matter, matter is particle based. On the other hand, the Basotho, together with other Africans, believe that matter is fluid based. This means that matter is wave-based and has wave properties.

This entails that Basotho regard any material in the universe as fluid-based and subject to the laws of fluid dynamics. The Sesotho language confirms this amazing fact. When the Basotho dish out food, they say "*Batshela* dijo" meaning "They are *pouring* out food" as if food is a fluid. When they throw away waste they say "*Batsholla* dithole" meaning they are *pouring* out waste as if waste is fluid based. The cosmic language of the Basotho treats matter and all kinds of material as fluid based.

This concept of fluid-based matter is attested for in the ancient manuscripts of Egypt which declare that in the beginning there was uncreated matter in the form of primordial waters. The creator then came out of this uncreated matter and began to create the heavens, the stellar bodies and the earth. All this was created out of a fluid-based matter. If you were to count fluid-based words in the English language, the list is not that long and the English language soon hits a lexical limit. However, the Basotho lexicon in the domain of fluidity goes to infinity.

9

As a result of their cosmic knowledge, the Basotho believe that the most sacred and fundamental geometric shape is a circle. They use this in their architectural tradition to engineer (*Horala*) and to construct (*Hoaha*) their built environment.

Through this cosmic geometry, the Basotho have always known that planets, along with the earth, were spherical in shape unlike some Westerners who believed at one time in their history that the earth was flat. It is also important to observe, in addition to geometry, the Basotho also boast fractal[5] geometry. They build their environment using fractal mathematics, something only discovered[6] recently in the Western society through computer science.

The Cosmic Knowledge of Dumelang

The fact that the Basotho possess a cosmic knowledge as per their genesis is also demonstrated in their greeting of Dumelang. Every time they meet, they exchange this greeting of Dumelang which contains the mantra of the cosmos.

The Basotho greet one another in a three-step process as shown next:

Person A: "Dumelang" (Hello)
Person B: "Dumelang" (Hello)

Person A: "Lekae?" (How are you?)
Person B: "Reteng, rekauthwa lona" (We are fine, how about you?)

Person A: "Reteng" (We are fine)

The above is a rough English translation but the chart below gives the real cosmic translation.

---

[5] <u>African Fractals: Modern Computing and Indigenous Design</u> by Professor Ron Eglash documents the African origin of fractal design, science and mathematics. The book is published by Rutgers University Press.

[6] The French mathematician Benoit Mandelbrot reported the first visualization of fractals at the IBM's laboratory in 1980 in New York.

Table 1 The Cosmic Knowledge of Dumelang

Greeting	Description
Dumelang	What they are saying through "Dumelang" is "We seek the agreement of the collective". The collective is the people. The agreement is the symmetry with respect to members of the collective. This is also mathematical in that the collective is the set and the agreement refers to the elements of the set. Thus, the greeting is a mathematical invocation of set theory. The other party responds by repeating the word "Dumelang" which actually says "We acknowledge the agreement of the collective".
Lekae?	Herein, they are making an inquiry. They are actually asking "Where are you located in the space?" This underscores the spatial existence of the Basotho. They are part of the cosmic space. They are trying to establish the location of the collective in the vast cosmic space.
Reteng	When they say "Reteng" they are actually saying "We are located in the space". This means the collective is located in the space, having resolved the location in space.

The Triangle Knowledge System

The Basotho command three types of knowledge systems namely (1) cosmic, (2) empirical and (3) theoretical knowledge as shown below.

Figure 1 The Triangle Knowledge System

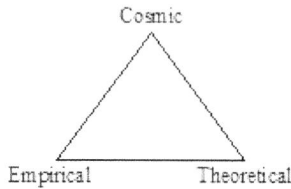

Cosmic Knowledge

The cosmic knowledge is about the genesis of the Basotho. This knowledge describes their origins and connectedness with the cosmos as confirmed in Dumelang. Before they carry out their agricultural activities in the New Year of Phato[7], they consult the star system of Selemela to forecast their season and determine the types of crops to grow. If the Basotho astronomers declare a dry season, based on the Selemela star system, then Basotho grow more of the drought resistant crops like Mabele[8], thepe[9] and others.

The interesting fact is that Mabele contain lots of potassium with high efficacy in the prevention and management of metabolic illnesses like high blood pressure or diabetes as already mentioned. When the Africans live in accordance with their cosmic knowledge and their traditions, then their health also thrives. In the village of Matamong, the people were so healthy they did not suffer from these kinds of diseases. In addition to the above, the Matamong people also enjoyed other health-improving plant-based foods like Mandolondolo, Tswekere, Sehwete, Torofeiye, Monokotshwai, among others.

Interestingly, cosmic knowledge is also a source of new philosophical constructs for the Basotho. A case in point is the planet Venus. Basotho have two names Sefalabohoho (Venus in the evening) and Mphatlalatsane (Venus in the morning). Sefalabohoho actually means "The one who eats the food to the crust". In this case, the Basotho use the behaviour and properties of the star system to refer to the star object instead of referring to the star directly.

Sefalabohoho encapsulates intensional logic[10] (*intensional* with an "s") as part of Basotho's reverence for the heavens. It's more reverential to

---

[7] Month of August. The Basotho calendar begins in August (Beginning of Spring in South Africa) and ends in July (End of Winter in South Africa). This makes a Basotho calendar a warm calendar in contrast to the European calendar which begins in January (very cold month) and ends in December (yet another cold month). This makes the European calendar a cold calendar.

[8] Sorghum

[9] Amaranth

[10] A distinction between intension with an "s" and intention with a "t" is in order here. On the one hand, *intension* with an "s" is about some word or symbol

refer to the heavenly object using indirection as an element of spiritual humility; indirection being an advanced form of symbolic reasoning as demonstrated by *intension* with an "s". Instead of referring to the actual instance of the object, they use the *intensional* properties of the object as referents. They are intentionally (purposely) avoiding direct reference in their naming convention in order to preserve their aweinspiring sense of worship for the heavens.

To assist the reader in better understanding the concept of intension with an "s" as opposed to intention with a "t", let's take a more trivial example. Someone might say something like "I need some wheels to get to town". The wheels in this case refer to a car. The wheels are the properties of the car object. The speaker decided to use the properties of the car object to refer to the car. This is an example of intensional logic.

Sefalabohoho also evokes a connection between food and the cosmos. The connection between food and the star system is an interesting one. Basotho observe food connection with at least three-star systems namely Selemela (Pleiades), Sefalabohoho (Venus) and Tosamasiu (Sirius). Part of the reason for this food connection relates to their food crops, farming and farming instruments as the result of their native connection with the cosmos. As a consequence of this cosmic knowledge, the Basotho consult the cosmos before they plant for the new season. Even their farming instrument Mohoma is designed and shaped according to the sacred geometry of the Selemela star system. When they need to communicate with their ancestors in the cosmos, the Basotho offer Mabele in order for that communication to happen.

---

referring indirectly to an object using its properties instead of referring to the object directly. In other words, intension is about the properties of the object. On the other hand, *intention* with a "t" is the state of mind with respect to some outcome or about something. In other words intention is about the property of the mind whereas intension is about the property of the object.

Consider the cosmic link between Basotho's food crops of Mabele, Mohoma and the naming of the stars in the following table.

Table 2 Cosmic Knowledge and Food

Star System	Food Connection
Tosamasiu (Sirius) star system	Tosamasiu has three stars. One of the stars which is invisible to the naked eye is named after their most important crop of Mabele.
Selemela (Pleiades) star system	Selemela's geometry is used by Basotho to construct their farming implement known as Mohoma.
Selemela (Pleiades) star system	Selemela is consulted by the Basotho astronomers to determine the agricultural state of the next planting season and the types of crops to plant.
Sefalabohoho (Venus) star system	Sefalabohoho is offered Mabele when she first appears in the evening.

As a result of the strong connection between the cosmos and food, Basotho perform a special ceremony using Mabele as a tribute to Sefalabohoho when she appears for the first time. In African cosmology, there is a perpetual causal chain between Mabele and the cosmos. This causal chain has a great impact on the destiny of the people.

Empirical Knowledge

The Basotho have an empirical knowledge system that comes to them through the senses. This sensory knowledge is a factor in their understanding and appreciation of the perturbations of the environment and the imperatives of adaptation. They use this empirical knowledge to solve challenging existential puzzles such as adapting to the causes of environmental stresses, mitigating the effects of environmental gyrations, and putting in place systems of counter measures to maximize survival experience. The Basotho consistently apply this empirical knowledge within their greater framework of cosmic knowledge.

It is noteworthy that the intellectual history of the Basotho demonstrates empirical knowledge as a body of knowledge that adds intellectual heft to their *Nahanotsebo* (theoretical knowledge). A specific case of such a treatment of knowledge is Basotho's observational investigation of flight mechanisms of birds in the village of Matamong which served as an epistemic case that transparently added more analytic understanding to their knowledge system.

Investigative knowledge of natural phenomena was part of the intellectual tradition of Basotho's school systems known as Motebong, Mophato and Bongaka. Bongaka was a graduate school of higher learning capable of producing a doctoral expert known as Ngaka and a multi-doctoral expert known as Nkgekge. It was Nkgekge who supervised the training of Ngaka. Nkgekge also served as a post-doctoral consultant for Ngaka. While Ngaka brandished a leopard skin for his doctoral knowledge, Nkgekge boasted several leopard skins as a mark of his multi-doctoral knowledge. These African experts were also known as Maaparankwe (those who wear leopard skins). The contextual poem The Teachings of the African Leopard in this book pays tribute to this pedagogical system.

Basotho's investigative knowledge is confirmed by their command of an incredible lexicon which analytically describes the different ways in which birds take to flight. As a result of this intellectual tradition and analytical knowledge that maps out the flight paths of birds through the heavens, the Basotho have enhanced their technical analysis overtime with constructs like Sefofatsepa (vertical lift), Sefofarutla (diagonal lift) and Sefofarapa (horizontal lift).

Sefofatsepa

In a case of Sefofatsepa, the bird effortlessly lifts itself off the ground using vertical lift. One of the greatest birds that masters this finesse of lift is the seagull. He rises gracefully like he does not need airspeed. The literary piece The Great Seagull pays tribute to the seagull. The diagram below illustrates this vertical lift:

Figure 2 Sefofatsepa method of takeoff

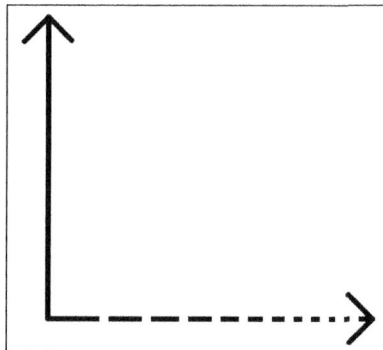

Sefofarapa

Sefofarapa requires the bird to generate some airspeed on a runaway like an aircraft. It runs for some time to gain momentum and then takes off. A number of birds use this technique like Kgwale (pheasant) or Kgaka (guinea fowl).

Figure 3 Sefofarapa method of takeoff

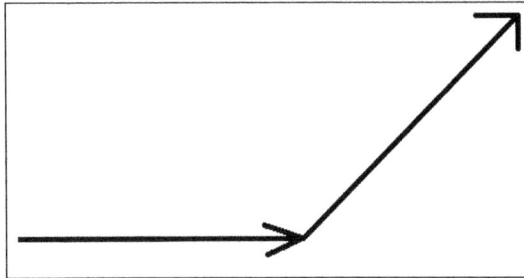

Sefofarutla

Sefofarutla is an interesting technique because it does not need a runaway like Sefofarapa. All that the bird has to do is catapult itself into the air and then latch on that wind current for takeoff. Birds like Maeba (pigeons) take off in this fashion. The suffix Rutla means like a spring. In other words the bird explodes like a spring before takeoff. The diagram below shows the spring-like takeoff.

Figure 4 Sefofarutla method of takeoff

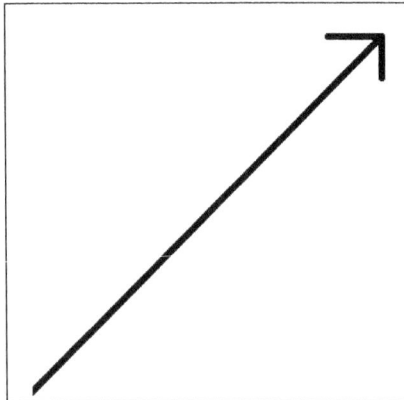

Basotho's unique case with respect to empirical knowledge represents a paradigm case where they do not view empirical knowledge as an end by itself, as is the case in a Western society, but rather as a stepping stone towards a higher form of knowledge. We see this form of higher knowledge encapsulated in some of their celebrated cultural systems like totems that bring together analysis of real-time data from animals together with African spirituality or their cosmic knowledge whereby stars carry names of natural phenomena such as Mabele (sorghum) or the cosmic connection between Mohoma (a plowing instrument) and Selemela (a star system).

This philosophical approach to empirical knowledge gives the Basotho greater epistemic access to numerical reasoning to frame their metaphysical pursuit of knowledge as encapsulated in their numerical artifacts like Diketo, Morabaraba, Kgati and Moruba. In addition to their gaming utility, these artifacts were also used as investigational devices for simulation or experimentation with a natural or hypothetical phenomenon.

Let's take Moruba as a case in point to demonstrate the intellectual and technological prowess of the African engineers and mathematicians on the African soil long before the advent of Euro-Christian colonization in Southern Africa. Moruba is a phenomenal technological artifact on account of its rare combination of numerical mechanisms of computation and gaming.

Given its rare combination of computation and gaming, Moruba serves the function of a numerical calculator capable of the five operations of Kopanya, Ntsha, Arola, Atisa and Kopantsha (*addition, subtraction, division, multiplication* and *concatenation*) together with a built-in ability to serve as a gaming console.

Figure 5 Moruba Numerical Calculator

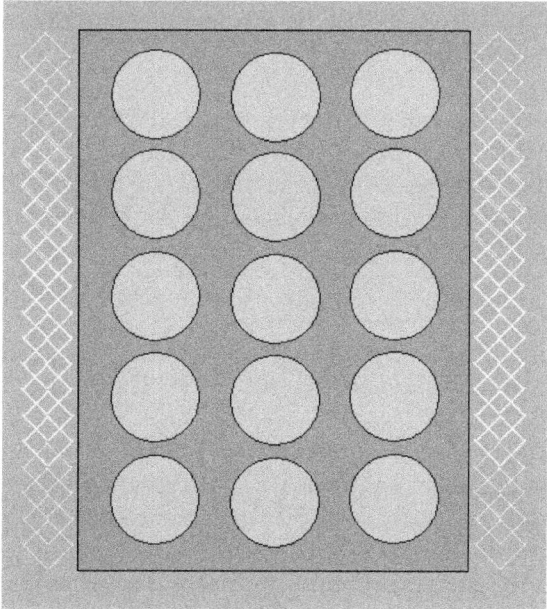

A technological device that enables utility and gaming at the same time belongs in recent history among inventors of European descent but the Africans predate this kind of hybrid technology by more than 800 years as confirmed by Moruba at Mapungubwe right here in South Africa.

This concept of blending a serious mathematical undertaking with a gaming experience can be traced to an indigenous pedagogical style used in the teaching of mathematics in the village of Matamong as documented in the ground-breaking scholarly paper *The African Origin of Mathematical Teaching and Learning*[11] presented at the Southern African Society for Education at the North West University at Mafikeng Campus.

Interestingly, the Africans did not harbor this numerical knowledge but they shared it with their European brothers and sisters. One of the reasons the Africans were more mathematically advanced than their European counterparts is attributed to the fact that the Europeans were still using the Roman numeral system which did not lend itself to sophisticated computation as was the case with the number systems already in use in Africa.

This situation only changed with the advent of an Italian mathematician Fibonacci (born Leonardo Pisano in 1170 AD) who had studied mathematics in Africa in the present day African country of Algeria at the Mediterranean port city of Bejaia under the tutelage of the Berbers[12]. Bejaia was formerly known as Bugia as recorded by Fibonacci. Fibonacci also studied in the African country of Egypt. Fibonacci went on to publish his book <u>Liber Abbaci</u> (Book of Calculation) which introduced a better number system in Europe in the thirteenth century. Fibonacci explains this fact:

"Almost everything which I have introduced I have displayed with exact proof, in order that those further seeking this knowledge, with its pre-eminent method, might be instructed, and further, in order that the *Latin people* might not be *discovered to be without it* , as they *have been up to now*."[13] Italics are mine.

---

[11] Proceedings of the 40th Annual International Conference of the Southern African Society for Education, North West University, Mafikeng, 26-28 September 2013.

[12] This author schooled with a Berber brother from Algeria at Carleton University School of Computer Science in Ottawa, Canada. This brother was proud of the contributions made by his African ancestors to world civilization in spite of those contributions not being openly acknowledged.

[13] **The Autobiography of Leonardo Pisano** by Richard E.Grimm, University of California, Davis, California.

The Basotho consider numerical reasoning to be the ultimate form of philosophical analysis and problem solving . This fact is confirmed in their axiom "Soro e thapa ka morabaraba" which means a difficult problem is better solved through a numerical solution. When Mosotho is overly challenged by a problem you will hear this expression "Dipalo ha dikopane" or "Haana dipalo" meaning respectively the numbers are not adding up or the person does not have the numbers. They say this even when the problem has nothing to do with numbers. This problem solving approach underscores the primacy of numerical reasoning.

Why is numerical logic so important among the African natives? What does this have to do with African philosophy? Numerical logic brings together three branches of knowledge with respect to the cosmos, spirituality and intellectual discipline which mathematics engenders.

Cosmic Knowledge

Since the Africans trace their genesis to the cosmos, such a cosmic experience requires numerical knowledge. The cosmos is located in space. Cosmic navigation requires a complex form of numerical knowledge in order to get around and survive in space. You must be able to locate and be located in space and be able to think in terms of three or more dimensions. As a native of the cosmos, mathematical grounding must be a natural part of you. The interesting fact about this mathematical grounding is enshrined in the Basotho greetings as explained elsewhere in this book. The analysis of the Basotho greetings also appears in *Basotho Origin of Mathematics - A Public Lecture* delivered at the Central University of Technology in the Faculty of Humanities in the City of Bloemfontein in the Free State province of South Africa.

Numerical Logic

Numerical logic serves an important function in African spiritual philosophy as part of the sacred numbers. When Africans prepare a sacred offering for their ancestral spirits using Mabele, a specific number of days like 3, 5 or 7 must elapse in order for the sacred beer to distill correctly for the African gods. This means that numerical logic plays a pivotal role in the quality of the output as well as spirituality demonstrating a rare combination of technical knowledge and spiritual knowledge. It is interesting that these sacred numbers are prime numbers. The prime numbers are also engraved on the sacred Ishango Bone[14] discovered in 1950 in the African country of Congo. The discovery was made by Dr. Jean de Henzelin de Braucourt of the Royal Museum of Natural Sciences of Belgium. The Ishango Bone has three columns of numbers referred to as **M**, **G** and **D**

---

[14] *The Ishango Artifact: the Missing Base 12 Link* by Vladimir Pletser and Dirk Huylebrouck in Forma, 14, 339–346, 1999.

respectively. The **G** column lists prime numbers; the first and oldest mathematical instance of prime numbers in world history. A specific case of oldest mathematics from the African continent was confirmed in my conversation with a prestigious Belgian mathematician Dr. Dirk Huylebrouck of the University of Sint-Lucas of Brussels.

In *The African Origin of Mathematics* article we read the following:

"In his scientific paper Ishango Bone published in the Scientific American (de Heinzelin, 1962), Dr. de Heinzelin states that the discovery of Ishango Bone shows that mathematical knowledge may have spread from Central Africa to North Africa. He further states that the world probably owes its greatest debt to the people of a small village of Ishango in Congo."

Intellectual Discipline

Mathematics engenders an intellectual discipline which provides for a solid platform for higher intellectual pursuits. Numerical reasoning brings about rigour to the mind so that the mind can reason during uncertainty and discover the relations, the functions and the syntactic rules which constrain the problem domain. It is this intellectual discipline that has the potential to deepen and broaden the horizons of an intellectual endeavour.

The erudite African ancestors who have gone before us carved Moruba out of a rock and used it in the African civilization of the Kingdom of Mapungubwe in the present day Limpopo province of South Africa as a computational instrument used during transactional activities of trade as part of the Indian Ocean mercantile system long before the advent of Euro-Christian colonization. The trade networks of this Indian ocean mercantile system included South Africa, Botswana, Zimbabwe, Mozambique, Malawi, Zambia, Kilwa and many other Eastern African countries.

At the zenith of this commercial centre in the twelfth century AD, the African engineers and mathematicians of the Kingdom of Mapungubwe had long developed a sophisticated technology of numerical computation as previously mentioned while Europeans were without a fully functional mechanical calculator. This changed in the 1800s when an arithmometer was developed and fully capable of the four operations of addition, subtraction, division and multiplication.

The computer giant IBM[15] confirms in their IBM Archives website that the Thomas Arithmometer was the first commercially viable mechanical calculator

---

[15] The reader must follow this link: http://www-03.ibm.com/ibm/history/exhibits/attic2/attic2_059.html

capable of the four operations of addition, subtraction, division and multiplication.

This shows that developing a fully functional calculator is a non-trivial engineering exercise. Even the great mathematical legend Gottfried Leibniz of Germany credited with the invention of infinitesimal calculus died having not completed the development of his mechanical calculator in the 1700s. Other science legends like Isaac Newton, Johannes Kepler and Lord Kelvin apparently complained about wasted time as a result of having to do simple arithmetic in a laborious fashion as reported by Cliff Stoll in *The Curious History of the First Pocket Calculator* published in Scientific American in 2004.

I have demonstrated the use of Moruba to astounded students at North West University at Mafikeng in South Africa using a portable version made out of wood with rocks in order to inspire them about the intellectual achievements of their African ancestors who have gone before them.

Theoretical Knowledge

Theoretical knowledge is outside the domain of experience and is also known as an *a priori* knowledge. Theoretical knowledge plays a pivotal role in the analysis, assessment and critique of knowledge systems. This also enables the Basotho to engage in the speculative forms of knowledge pursuit as is the case when engaging in the experimental investigation of phenomena such as causation, simulation, flight or any type of investigative activity that presents an epistemic opportunity to produce new knowledge.

The Philosophical Principles

Since we are in the African soil and writing about the African desert experience, we base our philosophical thought on the African origin of philosophy by the African natives. As a case in point, we draw from the philosophical wisdom of the Basotho who once lived in the desert in their distant past.

Through the stories, the legends, the axioms, the numerical reasoning and the puzzles that were shared with the author of this book in the village of Matamong in the Eastern Free State province of South Africa, we get treated to an African system of philosophy. Put on your seatbelts, as we traverse the new terrain of African philosophical origins of thought inspired by the erudite foremothers and forefathers who have gone before us.

The Definition of Philosophy

The Sesotho word *Nahanosene* as referenced in the <u>Sesotho Dictionary of Mathematics</u> refers to theoretical wisdom. It is the African equivalent of philosophy. *Nahanosene* refers to philosophy or philosophical wisdom according to the knowledge system of the African natives. The concept of philosophical wisdom in the Sesotho knowledge system gives emphasis to the dexterity of the mind as the baseline of intellectual endeavour. In the same way that dexterous hands can produce amazing works of art for different kinds of application such as therapeutics, a dexterous mind can produce analytical artifacts that enable the organism to master and transcend the perturbations of the environment.

Thus, African philosophy is about the theory and application of wisdom using a dexterous mind. A dexterous mind is key in African philosophy because it brings to the forefront the significance of thought-processing. This kind of philosophical mastery is fundamental to the maximization of the survival experience of the organism and the clan.

As a result of this epistemological system with respect to a dexterous mind, intelligence is defined in a more specific and articulated fashion. Suppose we have person **A** and person **B**. We give both of them an identical problem to solve. The problem that has to be solved is a novel challenge to the participants. Our criteria of intellectual competency necessitate that the one who solves the problem correctly must do so in a shortest amount of time. If person **A** correctly solves the problem before person **B** in the timeline then person **A** is the genius. This gives us a more quantifiable measure of intelligence. The test is blind to the cultural or genetic background of the participants. The only commonality between the participants is their natural instinct to gain a survival advantage. What is interesting about this objective test is that it demands a rapid and extensive memory formation from the naive organism about the novel stimulus which is key to the maximization of the survival experience of the organism.

We can also use the same brain processing test between a human being and a monkey. If the monkey correctly solves the same problem before a human being then the monkey is the genius. It turns out that the monkey has a better brain processing speed than a human being a fact that has been observed by the African natives of Southern Africa. As a corollary, poetic chronicles of oration have been produced from generation to generation to honour the great legends of Motshweneng and Mfene (the clans of the monkey). What is venerated here are the indomitable intellectual, behavioural and adaptive attributes of the animals which have become integrated into a sacred mythology of the people.

This kind of intellectual test is linked to the survival of the organism. If a naive organism is faced with a novel challenge, it must first learn about the problem before it can correctly solve it. Solving a problem before understanding it would be a survival terminating behaviour. Notwithstanding, having to understand the problem before solving it also imposes a survival constraint. The most adaptable behaviour obviates this double jeopardy by ensuring that the organism is internally directed by a rule that solves the problem within the economy of time. For this reason, the organism that requires the least amount of time to crack the problem gains an automatic survival advantage over others. Since enhancing self-preservation is a survival imperative, the most successful organism will go on to live and pass on its survival knowledge system to the members of the clan effectively ensuring the collective success of the clan.

The Five Constructs of Philosophy

The Basotho system of philosophical thinking is comprised of five constructs (1) *Koma*, (2) *Masene*, *(3) Sekaseko*, (4) *Nahanotsebo* and (5) *Kanamotwa* as referenced in the <u>Sesotho Dictionary of Mathematics</u>. In the English language these are namely (1) truth, (2) wisdom, (3) analysis, (4) knowledge, and (5) ethics. Using set theory, we generate the following set and its elements:

Nahanosene {truth, wisdom, analysis, knowledge, ethics}

Looking at this set, one might ask: Where is logic? Logic exists as a subset of truth with respect to the epistemic system of the Basotho. The modern Basotho speakers might also wonder how come I used the word *Koma* instead of the word *Nnete*. This is because *Koma* is a more scholarly concept than *Nnete* in accordance with the Mophato and Bongaka systems of higher education, which preexisted the advent of colonization. In other words, *Nnete* is a subset of *Koma*. It is noteworthy that *knowledge* is not a complete translation.

The Sesotho construct *Nahanotsebo* translates into "Theoretical knowledge" but for purposes of brevity, the theoretical part was left out. The important observation is that the Basotho distinguish between theoretical knowledge *Nahanotsebo* and concrete knowledge *Tsebokato* or *Tsebo Ya Mokato* something that will prove instrumental in our thought processing while developing a transcendental mind.

We now list the constructs and their definitions starting with the truth of Koma.

KOMA (THE TRUTH)

The Sesotho word Koma is a powerful concept. Koma refers to a drum, the ancestors, and an impartial truth. Using set theory, we generate the following set and the elements thereof:

Koma {truth, drum, ancestors}

The ancient Basotho scholars used the word Koma to refer to an impartial truth. The truth of Koma is constant and immutable. The constancy and immutability of truth are imperative for the organism to rely on the truth. If the truth is impartial, then the organism can also rely on the fairness of the truth.

The Sesotho axiom *"Hoikana ka koma"* means to swear by the truth of Koma. The axiom *"Hoanakoma"* means *"To forever treat the truth of Koma as sacred"*. An initiate who is called by the ancestors to become a healer will also have a song of the ancestors. When she graduates as Mokoma[16] from the doctoral school of Bongaka which allows her to practice as a medicine woman, she performs something called *"Hophokola koma"* meaning *"To invoke the song of the ancestors"* in which case she sings and dances to the ancestors. She pledges loyalty to the fact that she will always be bound by the truth of Koma.

The members of the village witness her pledge and the convocation ceremony. Another axiom *"Nnete ya Mmakoma"* means the truth of Koma as practiced by a female Mokoma. It is an interesting fact that even though Mokoma refers to both male and female healers, this particular axiom refers to a female Mokoma as the vanguard of the truth of Koma. In this particular case, the axiom venerates the truth of Koma according to the female principle[17].

The Sesotho axiom *"Monokotshwai haobutswe hoya ka takatso ya tshwene"* translates into *"The fruit does not become ripe according to the desire of the monkey"*. This powerful axiom refers to the metaphysical pursuit of the truth among the Basotho based on an impartial truth. Since the desire or wish of the monkey is not able to alter or expedite the ripening state of the fruit, the ontological axiom is also telling us about another objective truth as cherished by the erudite ancestors of the Basotho.

---

[16] A traditional healer.

[17] In traditional African societies that are founded upon the matrilineal social structure, the female principle of truth, cleansing and earth is highly venerated. This concept of female principle is documented in *Organic Roots of the African Matrilineal Society*.

There are seven laws that emanate from the axiom as shown in the next table:

Table 3 Sesotho Laws of Monokotshwai

Sesotho Laws of Monokotshwai	
Sesotho	**English**
Boimeteng ba nnete	The objective existence of the truth
Hochobakoma	The impartial existence of the truth
Hoanakoma	The sacred existence of the truth
Hoanamotwa	The sacred moral code of existence
Hoselaolwe ke ditakatso tsa nama	Not overruled by the desires of the flesh
Hothakgisa ditakatso tsa nama	To crucify the desires of the flesh
Monokotshwai obusa ka lerelatshepe	The Immutable Law of Monokotshwai

In African philosophical thought, the truth is a superset and logic is a subset of the superset. This contrasts sharply with Western philosophical thought whereby you arrive at the truth through logic in which case logic is the superset and the truth a subset of the superset. To demonstrate an instance of the African elements of truth, we show the following set:

Truth {logic, wisdom, state}

The elements of the truth set are *logic*, *wisdom* and *state*. If we generate the set of the *state* element we get the following:

State {impartiality, objectivity, sacredness}

The elements of the state set are *impartiality*, *objectivity* and *sacredness*. This means that the states of the truth are *impartial*, *objective* and *sacred*. These are very important ontological states of the truth according to the Basotho. The Basotho consider these truth states to define their reference knowledge of ontology.

Since their religiosity is based on ancestral worship and the cosmos which defines their genesis, the Basotho consider their religion to be based on the impartiality, the objectivity and the sacredness of the truth. In view of the fact that an ancestral god or goddess previously existed in human form on the planet, that means he or she does not lose the objective relation with the earth. The impartial truth (*Nnete eseng lekeke*), the objective truth (*Nnete ya boime*) and the sacredness of the truth of Koma (*Hoanakoma*) are core elements of the Sesotho philosophical thought.

The Sesotho term *Hochobakoma* refers to the practice and pursuit of impartial truth whereas another term *Hoanakoma* as mentioned above refers to the sacred practice of the truth. There are two institutions in which these philosophical concepts are enshrined namely (1) Bokoma and (2) Lekgotla.

Bokoma

Bokoma is concerned with healing, truth seeking and providing a medium of communication between humans and the ancestors who have gone before them. The suffix of Bokoma is "Koma" which refers to the impartial truth, the drum and the ancestors as previously mentioned. In the past, the Mosotho would say *"Keikana ka koma"* meaning "I swear by the impartial truth of Koma". In the African philosophy of the Basotho, the impartiality of the truth is extremely important. It serves as a moral code that guides behaviour, governance of the affairs and the relations with others.

Interestingly, the Basotho do not leave the concept of Koma to the goodwill of humans. They provide an independent mechanism that ensures that the truth of Koma is upheld at all times using a sacred artifact known as Lechoba and which is held by the one who swears by the truth of Koma. The Mokoma must hold in her hand Lechoba which gives her the ceremonial and spiritual authority to speak. She can never speak without Lechoba. The moment of holding Lechoba is sacred and cannot be interrupted by anyone.

Lekgotla

Lekgotla is an institutional system used to govern, arbitrate and deliberate on the affairs of the village. The mechanism of Lechoba also applies to the Lekgotla system. The Lechoba guarantees the sacredness of the moment when a speaker is to be heard. During the moment when the speaker holds the Lechoba, no one can interrupt the speaker. The chairperson of the Lekgotla must hold the Lechoba in the hand just like Mokoma. The Lechoba is there to authorize and protect the participant's right to speak in the Lekgotla system. If a member of Lekgotla wishes to speak and he does not have a Lechoba in his hand then he must hold his peace until the Lechoba comes to him. Part of the reason the Lechoba is so important is that it serves as a mechanism of cultural and spiritual symbol with regards to impartial truth.

The Sesotho concept *Bochobakoma* meaning "The practice of impartial truth" refers to the absence of selection or bias with respect to the truth, whereas another Sesotho concept *Boime* "The objectiveness of the object" refers to the inability of thoughts, wishes or belief systems to alter the existence of the truth. The truth could be a material phenomenon like a tree, or an immaterial phenomenon like a social event. The word "immaterial" is used here to refer to a non-material phenomenon.

Having discussed the impartiality of the truth, the objectivity of the truth, and the sacredness of the truth does it then mean that in the religious philosophy of the Basotho there are no miracles given the fact that thoughts, wishes or belief systems are not able to alter the objective state of the material truth?[18]

Let's define the word "miracle" to mean an event that seemingly occurs outside of or in contravention to the laws of nature. Some religious leaders perform certain acts of healing as "miracles". These "miracles" happen at the command of the religious leader after invoking his or her religious powers. The formula for such miracles goes something like "In the name of X, I command you to become Y". When the person to whom the miracle is being performed assumes the value of Y then the miracle has occurred.

The Basotho religious philosophy does not subscribe to such a concept of "miracles" as conferred on the basis of individuality. The reason is that the Basotho religious philosophy is a collective philosophical thought and things have to happen in the context of the collective as opposed to the aforementioned whereby things happen at the command of an individual. A Sesotho axiom "Motho ke motho ka batho", which tells us that a human is human on account of other humans, underscores the essence of the collective. The invocation of "a miracle" by an individual violates this principle.

The Basotho trace their origin to the cosmos. This means they are subject to both terrestrial laws of nature and the cosmic laws of their genesis. After the ancestors have left the terrestrial sphere to return to the cosmos, they acquire new powers with respect to communicating with humans. In this case, there is an interplay of terrestrial laws and cosmic laws. Certain things might happen as a result of the cosmic laws. The laws governing this communication between the terrestrial and the cosmic are beyond the discussion of this chapter but those laws exist and operate according to the Basotho indigenous knowledge systems.

There are events that would be considered miraculous and I have been an observer of such extraordinary events. For example, a spirited Mokoma might become a medium during a ceremonial gathering in which the ancestral spirit communicates through her an important message to the intended family. For those within the Bokoma community, this is not a miracle but a normal part of the ceremonial proceedings but to the uninitiated it would constitute a "miracle".

---

[18] In South Africa there is a strong Pentecostal movement in which miracles are performed by individuals. The idea here is that if the concept of "Monokotshwai" which says a desire or wish cannot change the state of objective truth, does it also mean that miracles are not part of the Basotho philosophy? Does this help clarify?

27

Thus, a phenomenon may occur under certain laws which may not be part of the terrestrial laws of nature.

For this reason, the "miracles" are in the eyes of the beholder and if they happen within the Basotho, they happen under certain ceremonial rules that govern them such as when communicating with the ancestors.

In his book Joshua Nkomo – My Story, Dr. Nkomo relates an account in which he had gone to a mountain at night in Zimbabwe along with others who came with him and upon arriving at the mountain a certain wind began to blow. They heard the voice of an ancestor talking to them. The voice was readily recognized as the voice of a particular ancestor who had long left the terrestrial sphere. The ancestor also recognized everyone who was there. This was a normal occurrence for them but a "miracle" for those who had not been to the sacred shrine.

MASENE (WISDOM)

Wisdom is the core of African philosophical thought. The Basotho lexicon in wisdom is characterized by great depth and breadth. The lexicon includes *Bohlale, Tsebo, Nahanosene, Nahanotsebo, Tsebokato, Leeletaba, Kamano, Kelahloko, Yakelello, Kgopolo, Fetatsebo*[19], *Yanahano, Paballo, Hlalefo, Maele, Dilotho, Mano, Maqheka, Malepa, Boquelequele* and more. In the English language these would translate into *Intelligence, Philosophical, Knowledgeable, Concrete, Logical, Relational, Cautious, Intellectual, Remembering, Saving, Idiomatic, Puzzling, Tactical, Tactful, Great Wisdom* and more.

These words define different aspects of wisdom. Using set theory, here is a selected subset of Masene:

English Set

Masene {knowledge, truth, logic, puzzles, axioms, enlightenment, relation, memory}

Sesotho Set

Masene {tsebo, nnete, moelelo, malepa, maeletaba, tlhaisolesedi, kamano, kgopolo}

Among the Basotho, if you are regarded as Masene, it means you are full of wisdom such as being *cautious, prudent, mindful, artful, astute, circumspect, alert,*

---

[19] Fetatsebo is an interesting Sesotho word because it actually means "tsebo ya tse fitileng" meaning the knowledge of past events.

sagacious, sage, sharp witted, among others. The word Masene refers to the dexterity of the mind with respect to its ability to manipulate the broad and deep domain of knowledge systems like logic, puzzles, axioms, enlightenment and others for purposes of enhancing the survival experience of the organism. Since the utmost importance for the existential activity of the organism is to uphold the law of self-preservation, wisdom provides the necessary intellectual vehicle to assist the organism's survival practice.

Given that a dexterous mind is the essence of African wisdom, it must be possible to break down a stimulus in terms of whether it inhibits or excites the organism's brain. The inhibiting stimulus must be minimized while maximizing the stimulus that excites the brain, so that the essence of wisdom can be experienced.

This filtering ability is an important attribute of wisdom. The natural environment presents a permutation of varying stimuli and unless the organism has the filtering ability to improve the SNR (signal noise ratio) of the stimulus, the organism may find itself paying attention to trivial stimuli that degrade its survival experience instead of enhancing it.

The brain of the organism only understands two messages namely (1) an inhibiting message and (2) an exciting message. Even if the environment bombards the brain with hundreds of varying messages, the brain must classify each message in terms of whether it inhibits or excites brain processing. Using this IES (inhibit/excite system) of logic the brain is in a unique position to make quick decisions in terms of the preservation of the organism.

The raison d'être for this IES is the assumption by the brain that the natural environment poses a potential threat to the naïve organism. Without a rapid and reliable way of knowing the environment and its perturbations, the naïve organism is at risk of sudden demise. For this reason and as a safeguard, the cell of the organism has been designed to detect the environment, to sense the environment, to adapt to the environment and to be triggered by the environment. The implication here is that the cellular mechanisms of the organism must be unlocked by the environment in order to function in a certain way.

As a consequence, wisdom is an extremely important tool in assisting the brain to enhance the survivability of the organism. Wisdom is an object that has the ability to manipulate itself. Wisdom can use other knowledge systems in order to maximize the survival of the organism which is an imperative of existential behaviour.

SEKASEKO (ANALYSIS)

Analysis is a keystone that contributes new analytical knowledge to our system of *Nahanotsebo*. The concepts alone without some systems of analysis would put the organism at a survival disadvantage. The Basotho boast analytical systems like *Sefofatsepa* (superset analysis), *Lewatsepa* (problem solving analysis) and *Sedikakgubu* (surround analysis) as documented in the <u>Sesotho Dictionary of Mathematics</u>. These are powerful philosophical tools used by the well-educated ancestors who philosophized and lived as masters of their own destiny prior to colonization. The purpose of analysis is to determine how an object or system works and what it does. Analysis allows an organism to apply algorithmic or heuristic techniques to unpack the contraption of a problem. This analytical knowledge assists the organism to correctly solve the problem.

Notwithstanding the virtues of analysis, it is prudent to assess the maximization of analytical knowledge. What we are asking here is: What is the maximum benefit of analysis? What is the maximum reach with respect to analysis regarding our understanding of the phenomenon? This is important in order to maximize the benefit of analysis. It should be borne in mind that analysis requires abstract rules in order to investigate a phenomenon. These abstract rules use inductive logic to bridge the gap between the theory about the phenomenon and its natural setting. Analysis helps us to develop an operational model that we can use to understand the problem better than before. The theory about the phenomenon is *a priori*[20] while its natural setting is empirical. As analysis progresses, analytical knowledge becomes *a priori* and thus removed from empirical knowledge of the phenomenon. For this reason, the analyst must carefully build the abstract rules so that the fidelity to the original problem is maintained. This may require a periodic review of the theoretical model in order to update the model in the light of new circumstances about the phenomenon.

NAHANOTSEBO (KNOWLEDGE)[21]

The Basotho's philosophical concept of *Nahanotsebo*, which refers to "Theoretical knowledge" as already mentioned, is a powerful concept that addresses knowledge as a superset. Another concept *Tsebokato* or *Tsebo Ya Mokato* refers to concrete knowledge. It is noteworthy that the Basotho distinguish between concrete knowledge and theoretical knowledge as already explained. These philosophical concepts are extremely important in this book because we

---

[20] The word *a priori* means before or outside experience.
[21] The Basotho preserve and perpetuate their knowledge systems using oral tradition, Ditema glyphs (also known as Nteterwane) and the artifacts of various kinds. A sample of Ditema glyphs is shown at the end of this book.

need and use these concepts and constructs to build a philosophical framework that empowers us to transcend terrestrial constraints of the troposphere.

Tsebokato is a concrete knowledge that applies to the operational activities of the organism. *Nahanotsebo* is a theoretical knowledge that is instrumental in the ability of the organism to transcend the earthly conditions. Transcendence is possible because *Nahanotsebo* liberates us from the operational fixation with respect to earthly existence. *Nahanotsebo* is applicable to the helicopter view of the organism whereas *Tsebokato* is applicable to the caterpillar view of the organism.

Knowledge is a mandatory prerequisite if the organism is to survive. It is also part of memory. Through knowledge, you can avoid mistakes, make better decisions, take the right path or recover from a wrong path. Knowledge is like a database that contains the kind of information that you can query and access immediately. In order to solve a problem, you need knowledge. In order to choose the right problem solving   strategy you need both theoretical and operational knowledge.

HOANAMOTWA (ETHICS)

Hoanamotwa is a vital construct in the philosophy of Basotho. Other related concepts include *Boitshwaro* meaning self-restraint. This is about the ethics i.e. the ability to discern right from wrong and act in accordance with the ethical dictates of conscience. This is about the mutual sensitivity of the organism towards others and the sensitivity of others towards the organism.

This also includes the sensitivity of the organism towards its natural environment. The organism must worship its environment since the burial grounds of those who have gone before us are located on the ground. It is also the same natural environment that provides sustenance which must be honoured with trepidation.

When the Basotho of long ago needed to cut a tree or use a plant, they asked for permission from the gods. This also explains the hunting expeditions of long ago whereby a medicine man or medicine woman was recruited in order to gain approval from the gods before giving chase to an animal. If the gods disapproved, the hunting was adjourned until another day when the gods were agreeable. As reported in his book <u>The African in Greenland</u>, Tete Kpomassie of Togo, now living in Greenland where he sojourned as an African explorer[22], tells us about a

---

[22] Tete Kpomassie created history as the first explorer to go from the South to the North. Traditionally, the explorer has come from the North to the South. Kpomassie has broken that mould to show that explorers can come from the

similar hunting tradition as practiced by the Inuit of the Arctic whereby the Shaman asks for permission from the gods of the sea before the hunters can throw a harpoon into the deep of the ocean. In his documentary *The African Eskimo* Kpomassie elaborates on his Arctic experience about the Inuit, how they lived and how they reacted to an African explorer whom they had not encountered before. Canada's TV Ontario used to broadcast this documentary when the author landed in that country in 1989.

The moral imperative reigns supreme in the life of the organism. The moral code is part of other rituals such as *Hoila*[23]. The selflessness that is derived from the ritual of *Hoila* is an important outcome of ritualistic behaviour modification designed to inculcate a strong sense of ethical behaviour.

The moral code must be part of the DNA of the organism. The Basotho philosophers say "*Haelesiyo mading, haeyo*" meaning "*If it is not in the blood, it does not exist*". This axiom employs an effective use of tautology in both the subject and the predicate to underscore the non-existence of any principle that is not part of the genetic code. By using a logical negation on both sides of the propositional statement, the axiom emphasizes the nothingness of any principle that is not engrained as part of the DNA.

The principle of the moral code with respect to the organism must be wired as part of the genetic code of the organism so that the organism is guided by what is in the blood. Another Sesotho axiom "*Habasaenyanya ke lefela la mafela*" meaning "*If they did not acquire it through breastfeeding, it is all in vain*" underscores the wiring of the moral code as part of the chromosomes.

Unlike the first axiom in which tautology is used in the synonymy of both the subject concept and the predicate concept, the second axiomatic case uses tautology only in the predicate and the concept of the predicate is not contained in the subject. This is another way that gives emphasis to the importance of knowledge as part of early socialization of the organism. The cultural environment is key in the programming of the DNA for an ethical lifestyle.

This powerful concept highlights the power of the genetic code. Why is the moral code so important? The organism must be governed by an ethos of ethical rules because the rules eliminate chaos and enhance the survival experience of

---

South as the African ancestors have explored other lands in the North in the distant past.

[23] The *Hoila* ritual is about selfless living. The Basotho practice this ritual as an exercise in selflessness. This arises out of a philosophy that a good leader must not be overruled by desires of the flesh. *Hoila* is designed to inculcate a sense of moral code.

the organism. One of the reasons nature is so good to us has to do with the fact that it adheres to a set of natural laws.

The environment comes to us with a high degree of chaos, instability and perturbations and as such predisposes us towards more chaos on our path. The organism needs some rules that allow it to minimize the chaos in order to exist amicably within the environment without being eroded by the chaos of noise, endless stimuli or caprice. The moral code gives the organism a sense of stability and selective judgment to keep away from harmful stimuli and injurious behaviour patterns.

We have laid down the philosophical framework that is comprised by the five constructs of truth, wisdom, knowledge, analysis and ethics. Using set theory, we have unpacked some of the philosophical constructs. We now turn our attention to the desert flower to embody the philosophical constructs.

The Metaphor of the Desert

The desert is a metaphor that models the setting of our lives in various ways. In the desert you are deprived of the things that must sustain you but somehow you must find sustenance from the same desert in order to survive and thrive. This deprivation serves as a survival filter to prevent the unfit from congesting the desert. The sustenance is there but is hidden. You must find sustenance like a hidden treasure. The timing is very important. Since "the fruit does not become ripe according to the desire of the monkey" it is a prerequisite to ensure the correct timing by the organism. This is where the organism must trust its instincts.

The organism is equipped with instinct and intellect. In a Western society they classify intellect as being more superior to instinct. In fact they relegate instinct to animals and assign intellect to humans. This is a misguided view of the two. The right question should inquire into the respective functions of instinct and intellect. Briefly, instinct serves a survival function whereas intellect serves a learning function. In a novel situation, you need intellect to learn about the settings of the situation whereas in a threatening situation you need instinct for self-preservation. Thus, instinct is designed to preserve the survival of the organism whereas intellect is designed to facilitate the adaptation of the organism.

The philosophical premise in the desert is that you must go out to get it using both instinct and intellect. You must not wait for it to come to you even if it is yours. You must go to it wherever it may be like the great zebras who travel thousands of kilometers to cross to the other side of the river in search of greener pastures as expressed in *The Crossing To The Other Side* in this book (*see table of contents*). The desert is not going to give it to you even if it is yours.

The Sesotho axiom says *"Phokojwe hophema e diretshana"* meaning *"The animal that survives is the one that is muddy"*. When the African puppy sniffs into the ground, you will see a bit of dirt on its noises and that is an indication that it is in the serious business of digging out a living no matter what. You are going to need all the senses and the dogged determination of the African puppy in order to make your successful mark. You cannot throw in the towel and say, "That's it! I give up!". You must dust yourself from the hot sand and soldier on. The effort required to get it must be greater than great.

Nevertheless, that is not all you have to do. In addition to the above, the awareness of the risks inherent in the desert must be deep-seated in your mind. You might see a cactus flower in bloom and decide to touch it with bare hands. Its velvet but stinging spines may rub off you and cause you great pain. There might be some wild beast that prowls on the desert and is ready to prey upon your naivety and vulnerability. A snake might be embedded in the sand not far from your feet. As soon as you make a wrong move, the ambushing serpent exacts harsh punishment upon you by injecting its deadly venom.

This is a small sample of the kinds of risks that surround you and of which you must be cognizant and vigilant in order to preserve and enhance your survival in the desert. By embracing the wisdom of the desert, adhering to the survival rules and espousing the moral code you will reach the finish line like a success story that everyone wants to hear about and applaud. Reaching the finish line will be a source of great inspiration for those coming after you.

As a philosophical framework, the desert flower gives us the objective truth which we can appreciate and emulate in order to become better human beings. These objective truths are confirmed by the Basotho who lived in what they refer to as *Lehwatata* meaning the desert. In fact the Basotho have many words describing the desert such as *Lehwatata, Lefeella, Nahathote, Lesabasaba, Mmananeng,* and *Lehlabathe*. This is similar to the Inuit people of the Arctic who have many words for snow.

The Basotho who survived the desert have provided to us the institutional memory of their experiences and expeditions. It is also important that we can distinguish between concrete and theoretical knowledge so that we can gain the necessary philosophical grounding in order to transcend the mundane.

There is a sacred wisdom hidden in the African desert. In order to access this wisdom, we need a crossing point that makes this wisdom accessible to us at a human level. Since this is the wisdom of the gods, we must be able to establish some means of communication so that we can hear what the desert tells us and we can also express our thoughts, wishes and purpose to the desert.

The desert has been very kind to us by offering the desert flower Mponeng to be our teacher in the desert. This means there is a desert school we must attend and the teacher is the great desert flower Mponeng. Mponeng is the native goddess of the desert. She comes to us in the form of a flower.

The Wisdom of the Desert

You need the wisdom of the desert in order to survive and thrive. This is the wisdom you are not born with. You are born with intelligence but the intelligence needs wisdom in order to work for you. You must find the wisdom in the desert. This means you must be patient, learn a lot, rehearse a lot and process a lot. Your challenge is to stay alive long enough to garner this wisdom in order to be equipped to survive and thrive in an inhospitable environment. Fortunately for us, this wisdom is going to come to us via the desert flower Mponeng.

What Problems Can Be Overcome?

What classes of problems can be solved by the wisdom of the desert? What is the problem solving methodology? How can our life be enhanced by the knowledge of the desert school? Who can benefit from the teachings of the desert flower?

THE CLASSES OF PROBLEMS TO BE SOLVED

Using the wisdom of the desert school, we can solve three classes of problems such as (1) the strategic class, (2) the operational class and (3) the tactical class. Every problem under the sun falls under one of these classes.

The Strategy

The strategy class of problems relates to vision, long term planning, goals, survival and governance of the organism. This class of problems requires the organism to think about the big picture and how it fits in that picture. It is about the big scheme of things. It takes time to see the results and this requires patience, perseverance and adequate resources to ensure success in spite of the lows and highs of the arduous road. The rise and fall along the way is a normal part of the perturbations of the trajectory. The strategy is about the helicopter view of the situation.

The Operational

The operational is about the things you must do to exist. If you are an individual, you need to pay rent, buy food, pay bills, provide security for your family, take kids to school and perform a host of other things that must be operationally in place for life to go on. If you are an organization, you need an administration, logistics, human resource, finance and a host of other things that must be operationally in place for the organization to go on with its normal business of the day.

The Tactical

The tactical is about the things that affect your immediate survival outcome or success in terms of gaining or losing ground, regaining lost ground, advancing or retreating. These are the things you must consider and decide upon in order to gain a survival advantage. When you succeed, you gain a tactical victory and an accumulation of tactical victories advances your long-term strategy. Just like the operational, the tactical is a short-term objective.

An example of a tactical advantage is when Alexander the Great of the Roman Empire was forced to retreat from committing his troops to the invasion of Nubia (present day African country of Sudan) that was then ruled by a female Queen Candace. The Nubians were famed for archery which was the best technology at the time. Alexander the Great was filled with trepidation when he saw the intricate formation of the Nubian troops ready to fight him with their projectile technology and a fearless determination.

According to legend, Alexander the Great retreated from his planned attack and as a result Nubia never became a province of Rome like Egypt. Alexander the Great together with his trusted military commanders concluded that the Nubians had a tactical advantage. Sometimes you gain a tactical victory when your opponent perceives you as having a tactical advantage. In the case of Alexander the Great, the perceived tactical advantage of the great Queen Candace of Nubia was enough to change the course of history with the result that the autonomy of Nubia was preserved.

THE PROBLEM SOLVING METHODOLOGY

The wisdom of the desert solves problems using the triangle methodology. After solving the triangle you are ready to be enhanced by the desert school. All humans who are able to solve the mathematical problem of the triangle will benefit from the teachings of the desert flower. There is no prerequisite of mathematical knowledge on your part. You come as you are and by the time you have read this book, you will be the master of the triangle and the wisdom keeper of the desert.

The Triangle

The triangle is a geometric shape that consists of three sides. The three sides of this desert triangle are (1) the superset, (2) the subset and (3) the surround.

Figure 6 The Triangle Model

superset

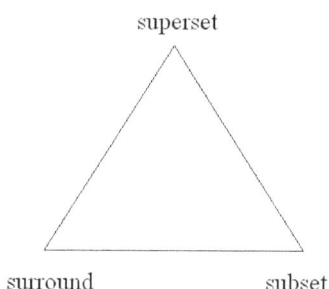

surround   subset

The Superset

The superset class of problems is the kind that pertains to your long term vision and strategy of where your life should be over a certain timeline as previously mentioned. The resolution of the timeline can be days, weeks, months or years. The superset is about a helicopter view of the topography of your life. It is about looking at things from a bird's eye view vantage point.

On the ground you see the sand, the dust particles, the drought, the cracked ground and stuff. When looking at the same ground from the sky, you see the intriguing objects like the landscape, the trees, the structures, the pleasing geometry of the sand and so forth.

The helicopter view forces you to find your role with respect to how you relate to the objects you see. You get to analyze how the other objects affect you in terms of distance, network relation, cardinality and permutation. It is overwhelming at first but as time progresses you will gain fluency in terms of understanding and using the helicopter view in order to increase your self-confidence and appreciation of this vantage point. Even as you descend to the ground, you must be able to return to the helicopter view to understand the configuration and the consequences of your actions in terms of fulfilling your life's purpose. You must also know how long to stay at the helicopter view before descending to the caterpillar view.

After gaining fluency on account of a helicopter view, you will then develop analytical, interpretive and resilient skills necessary to think and act correctly with regards to your peculiar circumstances. You will gain confidence and sharpen your survival skills so that you can constructively face adversity that befalls you or any kind of situation that poses a credible threat to the integrity of your being.

Once you have fallen into the right groove of things, you now command the mental fortitude and the readiness to persevere despite physical pain, mental

37

anguish or some pressing challenge in front of you. You are now in a position to transcend the constraints imposed by the earthbound existence. You are now like a seagull that effortlessly takes off to the sky using a vertical lift as if he is not affected by the gravitational pull. Once you are in the sky, it no longer matters how you got there. You are there and that is that.

No matter what, you must do whatever it takes to soar into the heavens in order to gain a new perspective on your terrestrial existence. This is how your spirit gets liberated from the constraints of this earthbound reality.

The Subset

The wisdom of the desert requires you to distinguish between the superset and the subset. While the superset is about the helicopter view, the subset is about the ground view but with an understanding that you are part of the superset. The subset is a caterpillar view of the situation at hand. This is about the operational details of being task oriented in order to succeed.

If you come across a particular problem, you first try to establish the subset of it. What are the segments of this problem and which segment can you start to chip away at? As you tackle and solve the problem piece by piece, you are generating partial solutions that will eventually solve the entire problem like a puzzle.

The Surround

The surround view is about the things that surround you since you were a child. The surround is about the unique cultural perspective that you acquired from your clan, community and family. It is about the way you were socialized and shaped by your environment.

You must reflect about your cultural environment and the impact it has had upon you. You must take the good things from it and leave behind the painful things that negate your progress. At the same time, keep in mind that the painful things of the past also present opportunities to innovate and reinvent yourself. A lot of good can also come out of an otherwise painful experience.

Understanding and appreciating your cultural background is extremely vital to your success in life. This also goes for the historical experience of society. If you are part of a society that had a painful history, you must be able to transcend that painful history. You shouldn't allow yourself to justify mediocrity on account of a historical past. Once you take your place in society, you become the master of your own destiny and the architect of your own fortune.

If you look at animals of the desert like the Meerkat, they live in a clan of many members. Each Meerkat is influenced by its clannish environment and this gives it the surround that will always be part of that Meerkat. When faced with a problem, it draws from the social memories of the surround in order to tackle that problem in a more determined and resourceful way.

The concept of the surround is very important because it agrees with the way an animal or plant cell is designed. The cell needs to know what is happening in the environment in order to mitigate the risks of the environment. If the cell is not able to have a reliable knowledge of the environment then it is not in a position to preserve the survival of the organism. This means that without some kind of cellular intelligence your life is not complete. As part of your life's philosophy, you must incorporate some degree of cellular intelligence.

Discussion Points of Analytical Systems

The problem solving and the triangle methodologies mentioned above are based on the analytical systems of *Sefofatsepa, Lewatsepa* and *Sedikakgubu*. We provide a more detailed treatment of this important topic for the reader.

Sefofatsepa (Superset Analysis)

Sefofatsepa analyzes a situation from a point of view of a superset. Everything gets thrown into a superset including our own situation and then we ask how we fit in this superset? How are we affected or enhanced by the objects in the superset? Is there a particular permutation of the object relations that affects or enhances us in a certain way? Essentially, the Sefofatsepa analysis gives us a helicopter view of our situation.

Lewatsepa (Problem solving Analysis)

If *Sefofatsepa* gives us a helicopter view then *Lewatsepa* gives us a caterpillar view of the situation. This is the operational level where the problem solving methods being used are assessed in terms of their productive outcomes. The caterpillar view allows for an optical zoom on the 360-degree angles of the problem at hand. Armed with this analytical knowledge, the caterpillar can choose the right angle at which to attack the problem more effectively. As a specialist problem solver, the caterpillar can repeatedly attack a segment of the problem in order to break it away from the main problem. Piece by piece, the caterpillar makes effective and productive gains on the ground. As a consequence, the organism builds reference knowledge which can be reused to solve new problems even better than before.

However, the specialized problem solving skills of the caterpillar are not adequate unless guided by a bigger vision that transcends the operations. This is because the operations are a subset of the superset. It's the helicopter that knows the direction. It is the helicopter that can tell if a new direction is warranted. The caterpillar can be bamboozled and bogged down in the permutation of endless angles of the problem and find itself wasting too much valuable time veiled by the grass of operational details.

The strategic direction from the helicopter view can resolve that bamboozlement and save the precious time. Sometimes the weakness of the caterpillar is to be overexcited and get absorbed in the problem solving activities on the ground even if it might be attacking the problem from a wrong angle. Sometimes the caterpillar needs to detach from the nuances of the situation in order to gain a new direction. Directed by a helicopter view, the caterpillar can turn its weaknesses into heroic qualities.

There are essentially three ways in solving a problem namely (1) applying previous knowledge, (2) solving the problem as you encounter it and (3) using a combination of the above to solve the problem. The type of causation with respect to the problem determines the approach.

The first approach is suitable if the problem has a deterministic causation. In this case, an algorithmic problem solving method is sufficient. A deterministic approach uses an algorithmic strategy to solve a problem because the problem has been previously analyzed.

The second approach applies if the problem has a probabilistic causation. The best way to proceed is to use a heuristic strategy. A probabilistic approach requires the use of a heuristic strategy because the problem has not been analyzed before and there is no previous knowledge to leverage. In this case, the organism executes some trial and error techniques and uses the partial solutions from the problem solving activity to refine the line of attack.

The third approach applies if the problem is stochastic. In a stochastic case, the problem has deterministic and probabilistic components. Even if the problem is deterministic, there might be an element or elements that are probabilistic. In this case we are using the third axis to analyze and solve the problem. A stochastic problem process is better tackled using a combination of algorithmic and heuristic techniques.

Regardless of whether the problem has a deterministic, probabilistic or stochastic causation, the organism must solve the problem correctly in order to enhance and buttress its survival on the ground. The desert is an inhospitable place that is neither going to accept the excuses of ignorance nor "my mother didn't love me" kind of explanations on the part of the organism. The organism is expected to be on top of its game to solve the problem in order to gain a survival advantage in the great struggle for self-preservation, freedom and advancement.

Furthermore, the organism must output superior problem solving outcomes in spite of the multi-fangled challenges it is presented with from time to time.

This concept of environmental challenges is expressed in the contextual commentary of Survival Advantage as follows:

"The dynamic environment presents new-fangled challenges to the organism which must respond in novel ways in order to gain a survival advantage."

Sedikakgubu (Surround Analysis)

The surround is like an aura that surrounds you and is always there with you. Others recognize you through this aural surround. You get the surround from your clan. As a Meerkat, you belong to the Meerkat clan. As a human being, you belong to some human clan i.e. the Buthelezi clan, the Fourier clan, and so forth.

The concept of the surround is like the Sankofa bird of West Africa. This bird looks back to learn from the past in order to go forward. Like Sankofa, you must return to the clan to retrieve the things that are part of your surround which you may have forgotten. This is where your aura gets re-ignited. The clan gave you a cultural template which they used in the past to solve the puzzles of life. This template has been in use for hundreds, even thousands of years. It has served the clan well. Overtime this template has been perfected so that it is the best form of modeling today. This template contains the clannish wisdom of your roots. You must espouse this clannish wisdom.

GETTING ENHANCED BY THE DESERT

After you have acquired the knowledge of the triangle you are ready to be enhanced by the wisdom of the desert. You get enhanced because you have now become initiated by the knowledge of the triangle. You now understand the three sides of the triangle and what they represent. Your understanding, appreciation and rehearsal of the superset, subset and surround of the triangle make you worthy of being enhanced. At this stage you have solved the triangle and now you can begin to harvest the benefits of the triangle. The triangle is now your greatest gift that serves you well in your life. In addition to the triangle, you also have the knowledge of the five constructs of the African philosophy.

BENEFITING FROM THE DESERT WISDOM

The prerequisite to gaining some real benefit from the desert wisdom is that you understand and accept it as a place of sacred beauty. Sacredness means that the primacy of your thoughts, intentions and actions is not about self-interest but about the benefit and betterment of others. Altruism is the foreground of your actions on this planet. It is the selfless principle that sanctifies the endeavour. If we think of others, do some good for others with no expectation for personal gain then we are on the path towards sacredness. It's the sacredness that will make you a beneficiary of the hidden treasures of the desert. The things that enable the desert flower to bloom when there is no water will be revealed to you and you too will bloom when there is no material reason for you to bloom.

As humans, we are earthbound and when we encounter adversity we become fixated on it and allow adversity to define our thoughts, bracket our thinking, destroy our hopes and reduce the size of our ideas. Adversity comes to us in many forms like physical pain, financial hardship, disease, lack of access or denial of access to opportunity, deprivation, lack of conjugal affection, going hungry, orphaned too early, bereaved, harassed, ostracized, exiled or subjected to a harsh situation that pins us down.

Adversity has this magical and chronological ability to hijack and deprive us of our basic happiness. Somehow adversity determines our life chances and future direction because of its historicity in our life experience. Somehow adversity causes us to be prejudiced against the possibility of a positive life.

The Sacred Knowledge of the Desert changes all that by making it possible to transcend adversity like a desert flower. A life of personal empowerment, victorious thinking and powerful batteries of hope can be a source of energy that powers our life and steers us in the right trajectory of victorious living using the principles, the teachings and the modeling of a desert flower.

The Sacred Knowledge of the Desert

The Sacred Knowledge of the Desert is about living in accordance with certain rules that preserve and accentuate the purity of the spirit. After the spirit is emancipated from earthly constraints, the body will respond by freeing itself from the things that frustrate it like unrestrained desires, uninhibited thoughts and static bias. A static bias refers to a fixation in a particular way or lifestyle without wanting to tamper it with some degree of rationality. An alcoholic, drug addict, sex addict, food addict or money addict suffers from static bias because there is no amount of logic or rationality that can cause them to pause and rethink the consequences of their lifestyle on themselves and others.

The body needs sustenance to maintain its existence on this earth but the body must disallow unbridled desires of the flesh of any kind like unrestrained craving, indiscriminate hankering, excessive consumption, instant gratification or addiction of any kind. A disciplined and sanctified spirit must not be consumed by the desires of the flesh or the thoughts of self-interest.

Like the desert flower that blooms with unblemished petals in spite of water shortage, a disciplined human being must exhibit an unblemished character and fortitude in spite of adversity. Such a human spirit goes even further by resisting the lures that take the focus away from the critical mission. Doing these things will ensure that the human spirit is enhanced on its way to self-actualization.

The Application of the Analytical Methods

We apply the African philosophical framework of the Basotho known as *Nahanotsebo* which gives us the analytical methods of *Sefofatsepa* (superset analysis), *Lewatsepa* (problem solving analysis) and *Sedikakgubu* (surround analysis). Using the principles of *Nahanotsebo*, we are able to gain an analytical knowledge using the above mentioned analytics.

Sefofatsepa (Superset Analysis – SSA)

Sefofatsepa or SSA is about a superset analysis of the situation. In the triangle, we referred to the superset which follows the SSA. The SSA gives you a perspective with respect to the objects, the relation among the objects, the permutation of the relations, the cardinality of the relations with respect to other related objects and the network analysis of the objects. This perspective is useful in abstracting away the commonality that exists among the elements of the problem in order to solve them. An experienced problem solver organizes the problem according to the skills required to solve it.

Lewatsepa (Problem Solving Analysis – PSA)

Lewatsepa or the PSA is about the problem solving behaviour. It is important to understand how you are solving the problem as this will provide enlightenment about the efficacy of your problem solving behaviour. Since the SSA provides us with the analytical knowledge of the kinds of skills required to solve the problem, then we can apply PSA to solve the problem. The PSA is a caterpillar on the ground ready to chip away at a problem.

However, a directional feedback is needed from the helicopter since a caterpillar may not know or realize that it is approaching the problem in the right direction. If the caterpillar is facing West when it should be facing East, then the helicopter will yell the instructions: *"You are facing the wrong way. Make a 180 degree turn to face East in order to tackle the object more effectively"*. The coordination between the helicopter and caterpillar is crucial for problem solving success.

The concept of Sefofatsepa analysis is also modeled by the great Hyena queen. When a cheetah gives chase to a gazelle in a high-speed chase, the hyena knows that it has no speed to compete with the cheetah over the gazelle. The hyena starts strategizing by analyzing the superset configuration of the situation.

The hyena knows that she has something which the cheetah does not have and that is endless stamina. She analytically follows the chase and determines the strategic milestones of the chase. When a cheetah eventually catches up with the gazelle, the hyena is a short distance away. She understands that he must first kill the gazelle and then drop it to the ground in order catch his breath before enjoying the kill. As soon as he strangles the gazelle and drops it to the ground, the hyena is there like a thunderbolt to take it away from him. The hyena is a flawless practitioner of superset analysis.

There are three ways with regards to a problem solving approach as previously mentioned namely (1) algorithmic approach. (2) heuristic approach and (3) combination of the above.

Algorithmic approach requires previous knowledge in order to solve a problem. This is a step by step approach that solves a problem in a given sequence using previous knowledge. Just like a recipe in making bread, you follow a certain sequence and voila you have the bread. What happens if you need to create bread called *Maqebekwane*[24] and you don't have a recipe? An algorithmic approach is not suitable to every problem because some problems require you to solve them immediately without any previous knowledge about them.

This is where the heuristic approach comes in. This is a method that allows you to tackle an unfamiliar problem that you have never solved before. You are not guided by previous experience but rather by a strategy of reasoning during uncertainty. In a heuristic method, you are guided by a cumulative present knowledge of the problem as opposed to a previous knowledge in an algorithmic strategy. Being able to reason during uncertainty is an extremely important skill because it enables you to develop a degree of fluency in generating partial solutions which eventually lead to problem resolution.

While a heuristic approach is an ingenious way of addressing new problems, this should be approached with attention to circumspect detail. The question of unintended consequences should be considered and avoided if need be.

The fact that you are solving an unfamiliar problem is fraught with its own risks. What if you are trying to solve the kind of problem that is explosive? What happens if it explodes in your face? The morale of the story here is that the

---

[24] Maqebekwane is a Sesotho bread that is created in such a way that it can stay long outside a cooler without getting spoilt. It is a bread suitable for nomadic travelers in a place like South Africa.

problem being investigated and dissected should be relevant, worthy of investigation and solution, feasible and ethically defensible.

Using a combination of algorithmic techniques and heuristic techniques can be a powerful toolkit that facilitates a productive problem solving behaviour in a stochastic causation. Indeed a better problem solving strategy is the one that includes both algorithmic methods and heuristic methods as part of the problem solving toolbox.

Sedikakgubu (Surround Analysis – SRA)

Sedikakgubu or SRA is a powerful concept because it taps into your particular context. The SRA wants you to incorporate your cultural context so that it can enrich your problem solving behaviour. Culture is defined as a survival template given to you by your clan. The template has got a variety of problem solving techniques and philosophies. You must draw from this. It is this template that has the power to suppress or express your unique approach to life.

Discovery of Desert Knowledge

With the merciful kindness of the gods of wisdom, we have arrived at the knowledge discovery of the desert flower with respect to the correct way of thinking about adversity and using the raw materials thereof to build a robust strategy of victorious living without being defined or bogged down by adversity. Through this desert school, we are able to transcend earthbound existence and achieve things that were not otherwise possible. We still maintain our humanity, but we are also armored like a desert flower so that nobody takes advantage of our kindness, Ubuntu[25] and humility.

The desert is a fertile ground for producing new knowledge. If you take a vacation to a desert like Kalahari or Namib and you take with you a personal journal whereby you will be recording your experiences, you will find that by the end of the trip you will have produced an incredible amount of knowledge. This is because the desert is like a midwife that assists you to give birth to a new body of knowledge. It is this new body of knowledge that will empower you, enrich you and equip you to deal with things that befall you like a thunderbolt.

The School for the Desert Flower

To survive and thrive in the inhospitable environment of the desert, the desert flower must have the knowledge of the two sets of externals and one set of internals. The desert school is there to teach these important concepts and the

---

[25] Ubuntu is the African philosophy of humanism.

45

desert flower must have the humility and eagerness to be schooled accordingly. We refer to these anthropic qualities with respect to the desert flower because the desert flower is a living organism and a dynamic life form.

Two Sets of Externals

There are two sets of externals (1) the superset which refers to the externalized relation of the organism with respect to other objects and (2) the surround which refers to the internalized relation of the organism with respect to other objects.

The Superset

The superset requires the organism to know how it is related to and affected by other objects which may be enhancing or diminishing its survival chances. The organism is part of the superset. It must exist amicably inside the superset while ensuring that its relations with other members of the superset does not impede its self-preservation. The relation of the organism with respect to the superset exists in terms of a network analysis. The organism has no choice with respect to its relations with these external objects. The external objects have an objective existence which the organism cannot alter through its wishful or spiritual thinking. The organism must accept this objective reality and then begin to understand and appreciate how it is affected by it. The organism can choose certain objects or take them out of its network. These choices affect the configuration of the network. The organism is affected by the network relations, cardinality, and permutation of the objects of the superset.

How Does The Superset Relate To The Desert Flower?

The concept of the superset is the basis of transcendence. It is how the desert plant is able to rise above adversity because there is a higher purpose. The adverse circumstance is just a small element in the big scheme of things and is not even a member of the superset. It is the organism that is a member of the superset. By staying in the superset, the organism can then shake off adversity and disallow any of its negative effects.

How Does The Superset Relate To The Human?

The superset equally applies to the human as a basis of transcendence. The human must be able to take a helicopter view of his or her environment. Through the helicopter view, the human is gaining critical skills in terms of transcending adverse conditions. Failure to take a helicopter view will cause the human to lead a life of a caterpillar. At a caterpillar level, there is no transcendence. The human must exist as a member of the superset and all other things like adversity are a small element in the big scheme of things.

The Surround

The surround refers to a smaller subset of the externals. These are the externals that move with the organism. They are only related to the organism. They are configured in such a way that they can suppress or enhance the organism depending on how it acts under certain conditions. The organism was socialized into the surround. These externals come from the own environment of the organism. It's the clan of the organism that determines the surround. The surround affects a particular way in which the organism behaves, views or interprets nature. The surround is part and parcel of the organism.

For the most part, the surround is friendly to the environment and predisposes the organism to act in a certain way. If the organism ignores or suppresses its memory of the surround it then becomes guideless and develops identity crisis. The identity crisis then forces the organism to lose a cultural template that was provided to it by the clan. Devoid of the critical template, the organism is now condemned to walk without a memory and forced to act by re-inventing the wheel of survival adaptation every time instead of using what is already provided for by the surround from the clan.

How Does The Surround Relate To The Desert Flower?

The surround is a survival template provided to the organism by its clan. The desert flower has the surround encoded in its genetic system in the chromosome. When a temperature exceeds a certain threshold like heat exceeding +30 degrees Celsius then the desert plant goes into a state of high alert whereby a cellular signal gets generated. If the temperatures intensify, a chemical message is sent to the DNA system to help synthesize HSP or heat shock protein. It is the HSP that will help the desert plant to cope with the heat shock. This genetic knowledge is part of the surround that was passed on to the desert plant to be able to deal with extreme temperatures.

Another case of the surround is when the desert plant is subjected to an extreme deprivation of water. When shortage reaches a critical stage, the plant releases a hormone ABA (abscisic acid), which assists the organism to cope with extreme water shortage. The ABA signaling also reduces water loss in the plant.

How Does The Surround Relate To A Human Being?

Unlike the desert plant, a human has two sources of the surround i.e. (1) the clan and (2) the genetic system. A human being has the members of the clan traceable through the community, village and the extended family system. This clannish connection is a very important link. The human must draw from the cultural wisdom of the clan and use that wisdom to inform his or her surround system. Even if the human may have become disconnected from the clan, the human must retrace the lost steps. In addition to the clan, the human also has genetic information that he or she must be aware of.

The cell is designed to detect the environment, sense the environment, adapt to the environment and be triggered by the environment. This is because the environment is encoded in the genetic system as a potential threat to the survival of the organism. For this reason, the cell is highly sensitized to the gyrations of the environment. For example, if someone yells at you regardless of the reason, a cellular signal is electrically generated which then becomes a chemical message dispatched to the DNA. A special protein is then assembled via the RNA system to be packaged via the axon to create a synaptic connection so that the yelling is never forgotten. The yelling person must be avoided. Notice that it does not matter whether the reason for the yelling was good or bad the harsh experience gets flagged as a serious threat to the survival of the organism. This is all part of the surround knowledge system which the organism must tap into in order to enhance its survival experience in an unstable environment.

One Set of Internals

The organism is forced to tackle situations that it is not familiar with. This requires a rehearsed and innovative problem solving ability. The manner in which the organism solves new and familiar problems is a function of its algorithmic and heuristic ability. The problem solving knowledge is heavily influenced by the knowledge and awareness of the surround by the organism. If the organism has with it a cultural template then this will enhance its problem solving ability. If the organism does not have a survival template then it must rely too much on trial and error which puts the organism at risk since it may not avoid or minimize those survival terminating behaviour patterns. The purpose of a survival template is to reduce over-dependence on reinventing the wheel by trial and error.

Conclusion

We have outlined the five constructs of indigenous philosophy namely (1) truth, (2) wisdom, (3) analysis, (4) knowledge, and (5) ethics. We have shown that unlike in a Western philosophy where the truth is a derivation of logic, in an African philosophy logic is a subset of truth. You must first be immersed in the truth in order to develop logical reasoning. The Basotho possess cosmic knowledge which has great influence in their daily lives such as their architectural tradition and agricultural activities among others. Their knowledge system is comprised by a triangle of cosmic knowledge, empirical knowledge and rational knowledge.

We also outlined another triangle with respect to their existential activities which consists of the three sides of (1) superset, (2) subset and (3) surround. We underscored the three analytical methods namely (1) *Sefofatsepa (superset analysis)*, *Lewatsepa (problem solving analysis)* and *Sedikakgubu (surround analysis)*.

Using the indigenous philosophy, the triangle, the analytical methods and the desert plant, we are empowered to deal with the challenges that get thrown our way and still manage to transcend them so that we are not defined by adversity.

Section Two: Transcending

The fact that the African concept of transcendence is defined as "undefined" creates a metaphysical case of thought provocation, forcing us to think outside the box. This paradigm case of transcendence provides a hypnotic suggestion that seeks to bypass a mental fixation of social conditioning so that we can take a disruptive page from the time-tested desert flower Mponeng who refuses to be defined by adverse conditions. For this reason, the desert flower adheres to the organizing principles that conceptualize about transcendence as being unbounded in the face of prohibitive adversity. Thus, transcending the adverse conditions is the highest form of survivability for the organism in the volatile terrestrial space.

The Great Desert Flower Mponeng

The greatness from humble
A sophisticate from simple
To grasp knowledge like hungry
To absorb teachings like thirsty
To know the desert to survive
To welcome the rain to thrive

To rehearse the rules of the desert
To grasp the gist of convolution
To conjugate like syntactic
To memorize like plastic
The great desert flower Mponeng
We pay tribute to the legend

CONTEXTUAL COMMENTARY

The great desert flower Mponeng is unmindful of the ferocity of the elements. Her schooling from the desert school has infused endless boosts of confidence. She regards the fierceness of the elements as their passion. She is gracious to the elements. She resists the easy temptation of passing judgment about the elements. She is the admirer of the heavens because they bring her the rainfall she needs so much.

The flower's armoury is the necessary shield to safeguard her in the harsh environment. It is incredible that despite so much adversity she is looking up to the heavens as the greatest source of love and joy. When others become negative on account of personal tribulations, the desert flower is positive every time she looks up into the heavens.

Part of the DNA

Haelesiyo mading haeyo[26]
Habasaenyanya ke lefela la mafela[27]
To exist like DNA
To signal like RNA
To be part of the genetic code
To code for survival advantage
To implant the moral code
Contained like DNA code
Rooted in the chromosome
Ticking like a metronome

Instant survival encoded
Remote sensing in the DNA
Unless in DNA sequence
There is no internal reverence
They need it in the blood
The code like a bodyguard
To program like the syntactic
To internalize the ethic

CONTEXTUAL COMMENTARY

The great desert flower Mponeng resists extreme drought in the dehydrated ground of the blazing Kalahari under extreme temperatures with no rain in sight.

Despite daring attempts by the desert to redefine her using adversity as a chiseling tool, the desert plant refuses to be defined by adversity and instead resorts to transcendence as a means of mastering her own destiny. The environmental stresses are not able to subdue the desert plant because she is genetically wired to transcend harsh conditions, exert efficacy of effort and look forward to the glorious appearing of the falling rain.

When the rain does fall, she blooms like a vibrant life boasting breathtaking colours, extraordinary petals and out of this world corolla in order to vibrate with the rain while rendering a dance in the breeze like a graceful jazz performance. Not only does she enjoy the falling rain, she also internalizes it so that she can continue to enjoy the rain long after it is gone.

---

[26] Sesotho axiom saying that if it is not in the blood, it does not exist.

[27] Sesotho axiom that if they did not acquire it through breastfeeding, it is all in vain.

Unconquerable Like a Desert Flower

To tackle adversity to the ground
At least to force a technical draw
To keep the eye on the ball
To reign in on the innermost
To contain unruly cravings
Never overruled by caprice
Despite sometimes apprentice

To gravitate like apprehensive
To fixate like adhesive
The invocation of *Hoila*[28]
Holaola ditakatso tsa nama[29]
Hothakgisa ditakatso tsa nama[30]
Hereafter unconquerable
Furthermore unbreakable

CONTEXTUAL COMMENTARY

The unconquerable desert flower Mponeng of the great Kalahari remains watchful underground listening to the slightest indications of the falling rain. The passage of time plays a cruel game with her expectations that someday the rain will come. Sometimes, a wild beast wets the ground to lure her out into the surface in order to destroy her. Unable to know for sure if that was rain or some trap designed to bring about her demise, she remains underground torn between her thoughts. Her deep roots save her because it's only them that can sift through the treachery of the shifting ground.

---

[28] Sesotho ritual *Hoila* refers to refraining from things, foods, drinks and activities which defile the sacred temple of the human body.
[29] Sesotho axiom for "To prevail over the desires of the flesh"
[30] Sesotho axiom for "To crucify the desires of the flesh"

Inducted Into a Life of Adversity

Burnt by a flame of adversity
Hot branded like a cow
To induct into convolution
To encounter intricacy very early
Adversity while uninitiated
Through memory hereby directed

It is deep mystery to find the answer
To be shrouded in the unknown
The support system missing
Solving piecemeal puzzling
The picture emerged like a trace
Unable to enumerate details
To manage complexity
Undefined by adversity

CONTEXTUAL COMMENTARY

The desert flower Mponeng was inducted into a life of adversity at a very young age. When she was transported on the wings of the wind, she had no ability or the know how in choosing her destination. When she landed on a piece of ground, she was exhilarated to lay claim to a piece of ground she called her own. She had nothing by way of earthly resources except her hope, fortitude and gratitude to be receptive and appreciative of the kindness of the beautiful heavens. It was here that she laid out her strategy of adapting, surviving and thriving under the most inhospitable conditions. She was forever in reverence of her creator for coming into being and she was determined to fulfill her mission in life to the best of her ability. She was an architect of her own fortunes, for better or for worse in order to derive her strategy and the computational knowledge to carry it out.

The Cosmic Egg

To gravitate to the sphere
To escape the exosphere
To reach for the ellipse
To cherish the sphere
To revere the cosmic
Even though like seismic
Hitherto my disdain
Hereafter my reverence

The *Seven Words* conjugate
The cosmic egg to vibrate
A freckled surface
Like a stained glass
Children of synthesis
Despise their genesis
For the sake of adherence
To create new existence
To deduct arrested gala
A deductive amygdala!

CONTEXTUAL COMMENTARY

When the Seven Words penetrated deeply into the galactic core, the cosmic egg emerged from the inner core to execute creative commands. The vibrational forces of the galactic core behaved like a thunderbolt in the cosmic atmosphere while Peo Ya Mabele (The Sorghum Seed) resonated strongly with the cosmic egg already entranced in rhythmic motion as a result of the celestial tremor of the Seven Words. The supreme powers of creation and renewal were venerated while the cataclysmic underpinnings of the inner core became restful as if arrested by the Seven Words. The sacred seeds of Mabele percolated to the outer space as if powered by the forces of the great twister. I pleaded with the collective of the creators that the souls of those on the planet earth were greatly parched for the divine words from the ancestors. How long before the sacred code of the Seven Words was revealed from the great collective?

The children of the soil were instructed to head for higher ground for a physical escape and intellectual transcendence from the stifling breathing space of earthly living in order to regain a new reach with the great creator in accordance with the special gifts of the spirit. This much needed transcendence would prove instrumental in assisting them to cultivate a privileged intelligence of seeing, hearing and sensing.

Thus the chosen ones to see what others cannot see, to hear what others cannot hear and to feel what others cannot feel as a result of a special gift of higher sensing. Transcendence is a prerequisite towards the salvaging and the cleansing of the mind, the spirit and the physique. The merciful creator is already engaged in the cleansing of the planet using cosmic rain to facilitate a detachment from the material and ideological trappings of earthly living in order to heighten a state of readiness among the earthly bound children of the stars. After a privileged communion with the great creator, I returned to our planet earth where I landed on a place of expansive Lehwatata.

As I consider the vastness of Lehwatata, the great desert flower Mponeng of the unrestrained Kgalagadi hides underground listening to the slightest indications of the falling rain. When the cosmic rain descends to cleanse the desert, she breaks through the ground in order to dance in the breeze as a tribute to the great creator. This brave attempt to transcend a parched ground affords her an opportunity to realign with the cosmos while fulfilling her mission as a teacher teaching us to transcend adversity and to improve on the destiny that was determined for us until such time that we can determine our own destiny.

Hereafter, to walk in the gutsy footsteps of those who have gone before us like the great legends Manneheng, Mbilini, Ntshingwayo, Dabulamanzi, Nehanda, Mantsopa, Madisebo, Dalindyebo, Masangane, Mqalane, Shaka, Sekhukhune, Mampuru, Modjadji, Soshangani, Zwide, Dingiswayo, Mamabolo, Ndlela, Mavumengwana, Moshoeshoe, Moroka and many celebrated sons and daughters in the land of the ancestors.

By renouncing the material and ideological accessories that use chaining to arrest their hearts and minds, the remorseful children of the stars must snatch this defining opportunity to walk on the tracks of their ancestors and thus to climb on top of the shoulders of the great legends who have gone before them in order to chart an independent path as the beautiful children of a great Civilization.

The Galactic Core

The inner core galactic
The spherical hypnotic
To fertilize the cosmic egg
To impregnate the celestial
Star formation near galactic
Despite inaudible acoustic
Hitherto, unworshipful and regretful
Hereafter, to adore the galactic

To orbit the galactic core
To venerate the elliptical
The powerful depths pulsate
To embrace like affectionate
Like kora masters offering
To vibrate the kora string
The great Mphatlalatsane
Traces the elliptical
In tribute to those before her
Undisclosed genesis guarded
In the great dark like blanketed

CONTEXTUAL COMMENTARY

When the galactic core revealed her cosmic egg, it became the most sacred moment in the great expanse of the universe. The sacrosanct cleansing was underscored for perpetual practice and strict observance. The galactic core entrusted the griots of the African soil with the celestial knowledge and the secrets of creation. She had the foresight to make this guarded knowledge of astrophysical genesis instrumental in enabling her sons and daughters to walk in the light of the manifestation of the galactic core. The vibrational medicine that ensued from the galactic core was understandable and accessible among the selected few in order to heal those who had walked away from the path of the ancestors. The great medicines of Lekgala and the desert flower Mponeng were highlighted as parts of therapeutics for the eternal healing of the trinity of the mind, the soul and the physique.

The unblemished queens in sacred garments of the cosmos danced to the ancestors in a ceremonial gathering of the spirits during a corresponding time of Mphatlalatsane at the foot of the mountain while observing their graceful movements a short distance away. I looked on as if arrested by their charisma while the revered Impepho incense sanctified the surroundings in the land of the ancestors.

The formidable vanguards of ancestral knowledge and animal wisdom guided the path of the healers while enforcing a sacred heart to every participant. The vanguards subjected Dingaka and Bonkgekhe to purification in the harsh cleansing of the desert and through a thorough-going washing in the waterways before qualifying them for the convocation of Hothwasa in which the graduates earned new titles as Maaparankwe.

Hereafter, the sanctified sons and daughters of the Mother earth were instructed to demonstrate unadulterated and deep interest in order to further know, espouse and perpetuate the authentic truth of Koma. They were further instructed to subject themselves to the rigorous rituals of cleansing and adversity of purification in order to walk in the uncorrupted path of the galactic core. In this way, they renewed their wings by infinitesimal changes to take off like majestic eagles to the great altitudes of Matamong.

Eventually, to persist a robust form of physical, intellectual and spiritual readiness as exemplified by abstinence, sacredness of heart, sharpness of mind, self-discipline and espousal of the spirit of the ancestors in a high state of watchfulness for a poised return to the stars of their origin when the time is mature. A periodic ceremonial state of Hoila is a necessary qualification for a protected return to the stellar universe.

A Delayed Aftermath

Abrasive distant anesthetic
A gradual present neuropathic
Acquired gradual numbness
To kill the sensation
To stifle the reaction
Unable to chronicle the timeline
To adjourn the response
To subdue like ballistic
The cuffs of syntactic

To delay the aftermath
Despite treachery on path
The killing of timely response
Like peripheral numbness
Fat ground for abortiveness
To subdue like elastic
Yet persistence like plastic
Despite a treacherous path
Yet to defer the aftermath

To re-awaken the sensation
To decommission the anesthetics
To regain a timely response
To bolster the loyal defense
Never to procrastinate
Hitherto to accentuate

CONTEXTUAL COMMENTARY

Like a bird with a broken wing, it is unfeasible to embrace a flight path. Even a minimum appreciation of a path towards a runaway is still not conceivable. If a vertical lift is not possible, the next option is a runaway. She needs a momentum and lift in order to fly. To stay earthbound shall forever remain an imposing threat to the survival of the organism.

In spite of the legitimacy of the machinations that delay the flight of the bird, the creature of the heavens must find an inventive response to transcend the constraints of earthly living and eventually lift herself above ground. The dark clouds are gathering and she must gain a survival advantage before nightfall. Like the great desert flower Mponeng who is forever listening for the falling rain, the bird must sense the first opportunity and take to the skies. The mental drilling, the physical discipline, the heavens and readiness for flight can only expedite the healing of a wounded bird.

The Broken Triangle

The genesis like a triangle
To evolve after an angle
We observed geometric rules
Unaware of entrenching tools
Hitherto, a broken triangle
Disconnected despite an angle

When connection they impede
The magnetic must recede
Chastised on Canadian ice like spruced
Beautiful connection was refused
A microscopic mind partitioning
Arrested angle to atrophy
Broken lines were connective
But network prohibitive

CONTEXTUAL COMMENTARY

The unfaltering desert flower Mponeng hides underground while awaiting the advent of the falling rain. Until the heavens persuade some clouds to burst and pour their hearts out, the flower must remain in the safe hands of the great underground for the coming rain.

The thunderous lightening has already flashed across the heavens to turn a page on the dry season below. The vicarious stallion and great protector was fired up to make the treacherous crossing across the fearsome waterways but the zebra clan remains behind raising questions on the timing of his crossing. The large body of water, like the great Atlantic, is now a fearsome divide between him and the clan.

Did the great protector cross prematurely and thus misjudged the crossing? This may very well explain the persistence of the dry season in the great Kalahari which puts him at the mercy of the harsh circumstances because there is no going back after the crossing.

However, the positive energy of the African soil is endless. The brilliant red sand of the Kalahari dances beautifully in the musical wind currents of the heavens while the electric heartstrings of the Kalahari vibrate energetically as if under a gentle plucking by the heavens.

Her heartstrings are like the masterful kora strings of West Africa which trigger a trance response in the heart of the great protector as he contemplates the crushing dry season below. Such an activist energy, which cannot be scientifically accounted for, refuses to be interjected by the harsh events on the ground as attested by the apparent transcendence of the desert spirits.

The desert flower is oblivious to such convivial ambience and thus unable to relish the momentous enjoyment because she remains underground listening intently for the coming rain. While the desert sands shift and dance endlessly under the infusion of the red colors of the heavens, the flower's patience is wearing thin as she religiously listens for the slightest signs of the falling rain. Is the much awaited rain coming soon? Who knows when that shall be?

The Obvious

The pieces were scrambled
The task was rearranging
The doable attracted attention
Prompted by the obvious
A hidden convolution elusive
Like a slithering snake in the grass
To make him sweat for the unproductive
To slow him down with the syntactic
To regain virginity of impervious
After deflowering by the obvious

Swift recovery like ballistic
Is minimized by the syntactic
To fragment the roots after deflowering
A golden finish begins to fade like brass
Having lost anchoring on the ground
The daring attempts at recovery
Curtailed by syntactic artillery
To solve the puzzling is inviting
Despite the clouds gathering ashore

CONTEXTUAL COMMENTARY

When the parched ground of the great Kalahari unexpectedly gets wet, the most obvious reaction of the desert flower Mponeng is to want to come out of the underground by breaking through the wet patch. Until she decides the right course of action, the ambiguity of the new ground subdues her initially enthused spirits. As she struggles to disambiguate the puzzling situation, her life hangs in the balance of wanting to be or not to be on the surface. The gravitational pull of the obvious is sometimes too powerful to resist the temptation of exiting the safety of the underground.

Nonetheless, she must consider the stringent consequences associated with believing the unbelievable and accepting the unacceptable. It is for this reason that she must trust her instincts and remain underground until she has complied with the painstaking process of disambiguation. By postponing self-gratification for future success, she becomes resilient and strengthens her readiness for the coming rain.

Uncertainty

It is early in the morning
Unable to go to sleep
Fixated on the mission for the gods
To pay tribute however belated
The myriads of unassailable challenges
Present a cryptic view of existence
Moreover social tyranny demands
A scripted existence
To make them accept
The unacceptable

It's enlightening to be uncertain
It brings humble feelings to the fore
To forever respect the gods
To serve their descendants however far
We strive to cherish them
To serve them before nightfall

CONTEXTUAL COMMENTARY

The legendary flower does most of her growth at night when the desert is cool and the hydrologic processes are subdued. She anticipates tough weather conditions ahead as is always the case in the noble African desert. When the great Mphatlalatsane of the heavens dawns as a harbinger of the coming sunrise, the flower prepares for the blazing sun that promises more extreme temperatures. When the temperatures far exceed the thirty-degree Celsius baseline, she prepares the invocation of the HSP[31] in order to survive extreme temperatures. The HSP is a fallback mechanism that enables her to buttress her loyal fulfillment of the supreme law of self-preservation; her fidelity to the business of living no matter what.

---

[31] HSP is a heat shock protein used by desert plants to overcome extreme temperatures and killer sun rays.

Fresh Rain

The fresh rain
Mixed with dry dust
To smell hereafter
Like something sandwiched
Between wet rain and dry dust
The cross mix
Allows fresh rain esoteric
Like selected tropospheric

The rainfall does not absorb the dust
Rather to marry the two
When the rain pounds the ground
The dry dust rises like rain mist
The water mixing with air
To create a white froth
To glide upon the surface
Like floating on subspace

The first drops of the rain
Dance on the fertile ground
While listening to the ground
When the rain feels the pulse
The rain spray rises with dust
While descending like a blast
To declare synthesis to the universe
We shall embrace like fresh rain
The sacred soil of the motherland
To welcome the coming rain

CONTEXTUAL COMMENTARY

When the first rain hits the dry ground, it triggers the wedding bells between the updraft of dust particles and the downdraft of rain molecules. The thesis of dust and the antithesis of rain create the new synthesis of lerole fluid dynamics or LFD. LFD is an intellectual terrain that embraces what it is, where it is and what it shall be. This is where the heartstrings and the cell membranes begin to vibrate to the dance of the falling rain to celebrate the heavens under whose command the rain is able to marry the dust to create a fertile soil and the resulting mud which gives birth to a new life. The teeming life is imbued with the advent of the fresh rain and thereby salutes the rise of the new synthesis.

Necessary Loss

There are times
Such as now
When I have to transplant
myself from here
To go to places never been before
In the process
I become separated
From the things that I care about
To suffer what has now become
A necessary loss

Humans like other organisms
Cherish the things
that make their lives worthwhile
The things
that are now artifacts of living
These things are not just materials
But they embody
our fears, concerns, appreciation and who we are
Throwing them away
is like throwing away an important map
Can we retrace our steps without a map?
Even the smallest mouse relies
on a scented guidance
To retrace her foot steps

Our strategic goal is to stay alive and thrive
This requires minimization of loss or error
If we are forced to separate from what we cherish
How can we expect the future to be better?
We shall find ways of mitigating the loss
So that we can be in tune with the universe
And thus meet the future with sense of survival intact

CONTEXTUAL COMMENTARY

When the giant elephant steps on the tail of a mouse, the survival strategy shifts from saving the tail to saving the life. The mouse, which needs the tail for balancing and mood stabilization, must now accept the real possibility of going it alone without a tail.

The elephant will not step off the tail of the mouse because he is not aware that he has trampled upon the sacred space of the mouse. Maybe the mouse must educate the elephant about her tail but how can she convince him when he does not even have a sensory experience of having stepped on her tail?

She must now incur the loss of her tail in order to live to tell the story to her descendants. This is a life-changing decision because she will be marked for life and will stand out among other mice. Will they accept her? Or will they subject her to another punitive experience on account of looking different? Could she have avoided losing her tail or was that a necessary loss?

To Transcend Negativity

To fixate by adversity
To yield to negativity
To lack the drive
To lose energy
The need to motivate
The need to energize
To transcend negativity

To escape the sandbox
The plant unable to displace
The instantaneous placed
Unable to exit unfazed
The plant like syntaxed
Unable to be faxed
Yet to transcend
Like never sandboxed before

CONTEXTUAL COMMENTARY

When extreme events like heat shock, cold nights and extreme drought seek to eclipse the desert plant, she remains underground like a coiled masumu of Matamung ready to spring to life when the right opportunity knocks on the ground. She draws from the innermost to find great strength to fight off the environmental punishment. Eventually, the heavens respond with great kindness to assist the desert plant to overcome her troubles.

The Glow To Applaud

Her presence unexpected
Her aura unconcocted
The aura's optical effect,
Ushers a glow, like refract
The glow to applaud!
The light source brightened;
highlighting the beauty!
A reserved smile ecclesiastic
The manifestation altruistic

The graduated light source
Punctuated like applause
The extraterrestrial glow,
A highlight of hypnotic intellect
Like the great queens of Nubia,
stopped Alexander the Great like inertia
Like a messenger of the gods
Unblemished by the earth below
To restrain like firewall
To serve them before nightfall

Contextual Commentary

When the sun slipped below the Western horizon like a red ball, the breathtaking moon emerged from the Eastern horizon like a majestic reddish ball looking even larger than the sun. As the moon wobbled like a giant sphere struggling against its massive weight to rise above the horizon, the spectators on the ground became entranced by the outer space spectacle of the heavens.

The Zulu mythology honours the moon as the source of doctoral knowledge hence the name Inyanga meaning The Source of Doctoral Knowledge. The doctoral knowledge of the moon refers to the superset of healing powers and the knowledge systems located in the galactic core of the outer space. This is because the African people trace their origins to the galactic core known in Sesotho as Mokgubu wa Kganare. The wisdom keepers of Matamong village refer to a mystic woman who ignites the fire of her brazier on the moon giving the moon the reddish light it has when rising from the horizon. The reflected light and the fire light blend in a rare combination to give the moon the exceptional beauty when viewed from the earth below.

The teachings of the moon require us to honour the air, the fire, the earth and water so that we can teach and empower the next generation to emancipate and honour Mother Earth and her waterways.

Section Three: Self-Preserving

The Preamble: To Enhance The Survival Experience

The sacrosanct goal of the organism, regardless of naivety; ignorance or unfortunate initial conditions, is to enhance its survival experience in the terrestrial space despite the perturbations that continuously seek to erode its survivability. To actualize this seemingly impossible task requires that the organism adheres to the congruence of the organizing principles that facilitate the outcome of a positive result. The organism must conceptualize about adversity like the contrarian desert flower that refuses to be defined and constrained by impossible conditions. In the event of extreme and prolonged water shortage, the desert plant goes underground to decipher the obfuscated signals of the coming rain.

Attuned To Her Survival Goals

To streamline like survival
To cherish like convivial
To inculcate a tunnel vision
Never more like scattering
The desert punishes the unguided
Hereafter to succumb like voided

To accentuate like spotlight
To underscore like highlight
A survival advantage emerges
After focusing attention
The rationale in accordance
Hereafter like transcendence

CONTEXTUAL COMMENTARY

The great desert flower Mponeng is attuned to her survival goals. While other plants are still struggling to come out of the ground, she is already dancing in the breeze. For her, the desert terrain is like a playground. These envious plants wonder as to how she is able to come out and enjoy the breeze before anyone else? She was the first to embrace the first showers of the rain. She was able to overcome her fear of speculative risk while others wanted to be reassured before venturing into the open.

Section Four: Self-Restraining

The great desert flower Mponeng of the expansive Kalahari understands that the self is highly volatile and cannot be trusted as a reliable springboard to advance transcendental moves against adversity. For this reason, she has a checklist of the things she must iterate by a process of elimination to ensure that the urges of self are subdued. It is a contrarian philosophy of transcendence that the self is arrested in order to facilitate the rise of the higher self to transcend the adverse conditions that pose an impressive threat to her survival experience.

Self-Deferment of Mponeng

The desert ground is wet
To extend the attempt
To punch through the ground
To break the resistance
The protocol is prohibitive
Like a drill surgeon,
To ensure the checklist
Before breaching the surface

Trapped by caprice and sliced
Rising, now un-enticed!
To defer the rush
To suppress the wish
To consider consequences
To consult wisdom keepers
Self-deferment like a tool
To yield to a desert rule

CONTEXTUAL COMMENTARY

It's both unfair and hard for Mponeng to remain confined underground when she can be showing off her ruddy beauty in the open. Nonetheless, this is what she must do in order stay alive. She must maintain a perpetual state of readiness while awaiting the advent of the coming rain. She is vulnerable on the surface without the nurturing and protection of the falling rain. Her survival advantage lies underground.

She has learnt to defer self in order to prepare for the future. Narcissistic tendencies can lead to a stunted and warped growth of self. She must be open to the universe in order to interact with it. She is part of the great universe. The ability to restrain self is the gateway towards greater rewards.

Restraint and Discipline

To meditate underground
To reflect before nightfall
To commemorate Manneheng
To pay tribute for her wisdom
Wisdom confers restraint
To restrain body's cravings

When governed by impulse
Unrestrained by a moral code
The cravings darken the coast
To corrupt the innermost
We gravitate towards chaos
When overruled by caprice
The rules eliminate chaos
Hereafter to live by the rules

CONTEXTUAL COMMENTARY

The sacred desert flower Mponeng of the great Kalahari is restrained from amplifying her rumblings underground for fear of being ambushed when she reappears on the surface. Moreover, she is under surveillance by some with acoustic instruments listening to the slightest tremors of the underground. She remains disciplined underground knowing that her emancipation will come with the falling rain.

Uncluttered Like a Desert

To be simple after reset
Uncluttered like a desert
To deduct the vanity
Excessive to extinguish
The overload to relinquish
The desert disallows excess
The desert to assuage
To remove the appendage

The tranquility of the desert
Refreshes like fresh air
The simplicity of the Nama
Hereafter to emulate
To fulfill the need
To expunge the want
Like a circle undersized
To exist like minimized

CONTEXTUAL COMMENTARY

The modest desert flower Mponeng must not worry about when the rain will come because she cannot afford to waste her strength. Mponeng will need that strength to spring to life when the rain falls.

Gentle Starvation

To eat small amounts
To starve afterwards
To refuse to indulge
To exist on a lemon diet
To cleanse like detoxify
To remove the toxins that kill
Small amounts now effected
A gentle starvation selected

To sample like a mouse
To pre-assess the impact
Humans overindulge
Unmindful of the outcome
Hereafter to cut back
Small amounts now effected
A gentle starvation selected

CONTEXTUAL COMMENTARY

The desert flower Mponeng lives a disciplined life of rationing. The scarcity of rain forces her to develop superior skills in economizing her survival resources. She only uses what she needs and saves the rest for rainless days. Her lightning speed in welcoming the falling rain is incredible. Although, she appreciates and adores the falling rain, she is very patient in waiting for the beloved rain. She uses the rain well and collects enough rainwater to last her longer. In spite of many distractions that hold sway over the desert, she is able to remain impervious to powerful influences like a duck of Matamong that dives many times into the deep water but still manages to remain dry for the most part. How is that possible?

The Strange Mix of Restraint and Patience

To restrain
To remain
To reverse fulfillment
To curtail excitation
To be serene
To wait like a hawk
The strange mix
Of restraint and patience

They are rushed like pressurized
Unmindful like motorized
The self they pursue
Like current unstoppable
Hitherto like probabilistic
Hereafter like deterministic
To embrace the strange mix
Of restraint and patience

CONTEXTUAL COMMENTARY

Restraint together with patience is a strange mix. They are both biased towards each other. There does not seem to be any checks and balances with respect to these qualities. It seems like too much to bear for the organism. Why does the desert flower tamper her life in this way? She seems to be boxed in by these qualities of constraint. Does this mean that constraint is the single most important thing in survival situations? Does it mean that constraint lends a survival advantage?

The brain of the organism is suspended in the CSF fluid system. If it were to be placed on some solid place, the brain would become destroyed under its own weight. The perfect place for the brain is to be suspended in some fluid medium. In addition to this observation, the mood of the organism is governed by brain chemistry that is comprised by chemical messengers known as neurotransmitters.

This system of chemical messengers regulates the mood of the organism. Some of the chemical messengers include serotonin, dopamine, endorphins, epinephrine, GABA and others with varying chemical functions. It turns out that the GABA system of chemical messaging is the largest of them all comprising more than 50% of the brain chemistry. The primary function of GABA is to restrain the excitation of the neurons. If the GABA system malfunctions the organism develops conditions like anxiety, depression and other states of destabilization.

This tells us that restraint is the single most important function in the brain of the organism in order to maximize its survival experience. This resonates with the Basotho's ritual of Hoila whose primary function is the restraint of excitation, desires and other physical urges.

If this be the case, the statistical probability of self-preservation is enhanced by self-restraint and patient waiting. Interestingly, we have observed that the desert flower is like a hawk in spotting the right opportunity to break through the surface in order to embrace the heavens who bring about the much needed rain.

To Arrest Self-Interest

To arrest self-interest
To subdue the urges of the flesh
To act on behalf of the clan
Unswayed by narcissistic
Sacred like Eucharistic

The collective reigns supreme
To safeguard collective interest
Self-interest arrested
To usher selflessness
Hitherto to embrace a moral code
To serve the collective
To arrest self-interest

CONTEXTUAL COMMENTARY

The great Mponeng has been schooled to arrest self-interest in order to pay tribute to the heavens. She leads an exemplary life of economy, parsimony, and minimalism and yet packs lots of energy in breaking the ground to dance on the surface.

In order for the Hyena queen to successfully reclaim the territory from the lion pride, she must arrest self-interest in order to act in the interest of the Hyena clan. It is the arrested self-interest that leads to the accelerated plan of attack on the lion pride.

Through patience and intelligence gathering, she now knows everything she needs to know in addition to having bolstered her foot soldiers on the ground. She understands that it is not possible to achieve permanent liberation based on unbridled self-interest.

To Overrule Desires of the flesh

To exist like diluted
To gravitate like directed
To refresh like effervescent
Oblivious to everything else
outside the inner circle
Bounded by self-interest
To exist like narcissistic
To direct like deterministic
Unaware of the superset
Uninformed of other's needs

The desert is uncluttered
Keeping only the essence
To invoke regimentation
To overrule the hankering
To subdue the craving
Tendencies like narcissistic
To subdue like masochistic
To overrule desires of the flesh

CONTEXTUAL COMMENTARY

She follows the traditions of Hoila which requires the organism to reign over the desires of the flesh. The Basotho royalty regard uncontrollable urges to constitute serious flaw in the character of the organism. Mponeng has been socialized into this tradition of self-restraint, denial of self, restraining the urges in order to become a master of her destiny.

A Rare Combination

Hot pink like gentle fire
Decked as if to inspire
To make the heart warm
To adorn a beautiful form
To be forever heartwarming
Even though unseen before
The physique like a golden sun
Is pleasing to the eye
But blinding to behold
Despite trying to be bold
The restraint of the syntactic
Solidifies like volcanic

Induced by beauty's refrain
Blending of beauty and brain
A flawless curvature is galore
Must resist to avoid disfigurement
For now to embrace curtailment
Devoid of self-interest that sticks like glue
To obey the gravitational pull
To resist like the great Sitting Bull
In his tribute to the Great Spirit
To observe perils of disfigurement
While approaching the pearls by the water
Even though the water will engulf

CONTEXTUAL COMMENTARY

When the moon glowed like a red ball, it was unfeasible to resist the gentle attraction of the gravitational pull. She commanded like a majestic globe while rising soothingly above the horizon. The surface was like texture mapped to highlight the glow that inspired a sense of a worshipful approach.

It was appealing to advance to the moon's surface for purposes of exploring and admiring the lunar morphology but the anxious feeling of gravitating towards the galactic core was prohibitive. To admire the moon by the sea is death defying because her gravitational pull equally amplifies the amplitude of the rolling waves in whose body of water the admirer will be contained. Is it possible and commendable to traverse the waterways of the moon?

The Great Mother Ant

The great underground she constructs
To resist power that corrupts
When new offspring arrive
They are well defended
Schooled in the teachings
Of the antiestablishment
The collective is interested
While self-interest arrested

They learn about altruistic
To commit like genetic
To uphold ancient wisdom
Like the great mother ant

When sovereignty is breached
Sterile soldiers must be reached
To defend the great mother ant
To preserve their cherished value
They repel foreign occupation
To regain territorial honor
To serve the great mother ant

CONTEXTUAL COMMENTARY

The queen ant is the supreme ruler of the underground chambers of the ant colony. She chooses and pre-determines the social and functional roles of the ants. In her great wisdom, she has determined that ants that carry out critical functions like food resources and military defense are fundamentally sterile. Interestingly, these individuals who serve the ant society in the sectors of the economy and military defense are expressly devoid of self-interest. They get vetted of self-interest while still in the womb of their mother. This makes sense because a mother's language and her environment do influence a human baby while inside its mother's womb. Analytically, sterile ants make better defenders of the ant society because they uphold the norms and values of their society without fear or favour. They are superior economic producers of their society. Sterile soldiers, workers, porters, janitors, among others, translate into a human concept of selflessness. Such individuals are incapable of self-interest.

The ant society highly values the attributes of selfless service. Self-interest, in which a member of society puts his or her personal desires ahead of social service would have his or her membership revoked and kicked out of the ant society. In a worse case, such an individual would be sentenced to public execution because the ant society cannot tolerate self-interest. Why is that? The ant society regards self-interest as an antagonistic contradiction of their way of life. Self-interest is

81

treated like treason, a betrayal of their society. A society cannot advance, thrive or prosper if those who serve in it are governed by self-interest. They must be sterilized of any traces of self-interest in order to contribute greatly to the wellbeing of others using the Sesotho philosophy of Bonyopa (the process of sterilization).

Colonial conquest was achieved primarily with the help of guns, foreign religion and self-interest. The modern popular media use this idea to perpetuate self-interest among the colonized so that the society remains trapped in an infinite state of a stalemate with respect to radical transformation and economic emancipation. There is a lot of talk about transformation but very little to show for it. There is a lot of talk about Ubuntu but very little evidence on the ground. The greatest question is: are we ready to learn from the great mother ant or do we remain loyal to the status quo that robs the society of economic emancipation? What are the consequences of self-interest for future generations?

I Struggle I Celebrate

The paradoxical struggle
The epitome of my existence
To struggle and to celebrate
To celebrate while struggling
To struggle while celebrating
I struggle I celebrate

To be stymied while on the march
To slow me down when moving too fast
The paradox is all I inherited
Generations inherit the same,
Dishonor of immutable shame
Despite tyranny we must celebrate
Infinitesimal steps towards a new slate
To refashion a better fate
Deliverance via the slate
Despite subdued by the chains

Contextual Commentary

When the dehydrated ground sucked every little water left, the desert plant could not postpone the important work of budding. The waterlessness was enough reason to adjourn until another day when the conditions were more favourable but the desert plant did not want to take the risk of doing nothing. She began to break through the ground because she couldn't wait for another rainfall. The green buds that showed through the cracked ground looked like futile at first but that was the beginning of a miracle. As the stems increased in size and the fragile buds waved in the breeze, the heavens looked on with great amazement that the desert plant was able to rise above the harsh conditions. The desert plant had sprung to life knowing that the heavens would send another rainfall. When that rain hits the ground, she will be ready to welcome the falling rain.

Section Five: A Glorious Appearing

When the rains fall from the merciful heavens, it is like a phenomenal glorious appearing for the indefatigable desert flower that has been lying in wait for too long for the life-giving precipitation. This is possible because the desert flower Mponeng is forever congruent with the cosmic resonance as a result of stringent adherence to the organizing principles that eliminate chaotic thinking to enhance the survival experience in the terrestrial space. She is like possessed by a trancelike state when the rain does fall.

A Tribute To The Rain

To salute the rain
To address a fitting tribute
The rendition is engaging
A tribute after the rain
Despite the battering
By the heavy downpour
Yet to salute the heavens
To be forever gracious
To the rain that fell

The mantra of the positive
Preserves the photosensitive
A salutation to the rain that fell
Signals grace to the heavens
The next rain shall be kinder
To accentuate the tribute received

CONTEXTUAL COMMENTARY

The flower pays tribute to the rain as she struggles to unfold her battered petals. She reasons that there was no way around this necessary sacrifice. Like the graduates of Mophato in the Free State province of South Africa, the desert flower celebrates her experience as if after the graduation ceremony. She has indeed graduated from the harsh experience of the elements. Her self-esteem is enhanced by the experience as well as the surround.

The Mother Was Not There

When it rained upon her
The downpour hitting hard
The lightening flick
The thundering thunderbolt
Mponeng alone in the rain
Unable to restrain the rain

When rainwater fell upon her
She absorbed as if to concur
Unable to defend
The rain refused to relent
The unrestrained rain
The mother was not there

Contextual Commentary

It is a good thing her mother was not there. She would have intervened spoiling the whole experience as it would not have been easy to stomach the lashing of her beautiful baby in the fury of the winds and the hardhearted battering by the falling rain even though she understands the mandatory curriculum of the desert school.

It is gracious to draw attention to the fact that there is no nefarious intent on the part of the winds or the falling rain or the dust particles. They are merely discharging their duties as per the exact instructions of the heavens. Eventually, the desert flower Mponeng has survived the downpour to become the greatest and most polished heroine among her peers.

Waiting Without Knowing

To await the rainfall
To be patient for coming
To wonder if it is coming
To wander about waiting
The schedule not available
The waiting like hit and miss
Waiting without knowing

Like the gazelle in labour pains
She retreats into the unknown
To hide the fact the baby is coming
The predator must not know
Lest they fall prey like preempted
Not knowing is the positive
To deny the inquisitive
The survival of the fetus
Requires defensive hiatus

CONTEXTUAL COMMENTARY

Waiting for something you care about without knowing how long you have to wait is most painful but without the physical sensation of pain. The desert flower, however, is able to wait without accentuating the cruel expectations of having to wait. It's especially hard to wait for something you have never seen. This is exactly what the virgin flower has to contend with; having to wait for the rain she has never seen or experienced. She must trust her instincts that this she must do in order to dance and flourish in the rain. Many doubtful thoughts cross and crisscross her young mind. Unable to know for sure if she must wait, she waits anyways. When the clouds of the heavens pour their heart out, she breaks into the surface excited about the falling rain. As the winds that guard the rain batter anything nearby, she learns the hard way to obey the winds and to await their directive before approaching the rain.

Maruapula

Like a promising future
Like expectant heavens
Promising to give birth to the rain
The gender of the rain unknown
A nurturing rain
Or a thrashing rain
To be known when it comes down

Maruapula like pristine
To signal the truth
She pours her heart out
A good faith attempt to be true
In spite of the apparent risk
Of being too open

Maruapula is irresistible
Like a hybrid beauty somewhat arcane
The beauty and the paradox
To impress upon the observer
Her discipline and work ethic
Her natural beauty and brains
Make it hard to shake her off
The observer must pay tribute to her
Despite a self-inflicted scar
To cherish her despite getting scarred
A paradox impossible to ignore

CONTEXTUAL COMMENTARY

When the clouds assembled to unlock the rainfall, the sunlight departed like a red ball below the horizon. For a moment it was dark like a melancholy occasion. The lingering moon was not invited because of her nocturnal activities despite exerting a gravitational pull upon the ocean waters. The clouds could not deny the moon because of her part in the hydrologic process. Eventually the rains fell upon the desert and the plants below became alive. After the rainfall, the clouds dispersed and the gentle moon rose from the horizon like a soothing red disk that sparkled. The graduated colours of red, orange, yellow and soft pink enriched the appearance of the moon across the sky. The moonlight brightened the desert below energizing the nocturnal creatures and plants below.

The Desert Corolla

Despite a low rainfall
Despite a dehydrated ground
Despite sun rays that kill
She rises from the waterless
Unimpeded by soil eroded
The brilliant petals uncorroded
To succeed like great Harlem
As if there was no problem

Despite dehydrated
Despite unmitigated
Despite losing ground
She assembles the corolla
Like liberators in Angola
To arise like Amharic
Despite killer ballistic
The serene unbounded
A sanctuary like ajar

CONTEXTUAL COMMENTARY

When the desert flower attempted to bloom, the scorching heat sucked every little moisture needed for the nascent buds. The water on the surface was nowhere to be found after rainfall. The hiccups along the way did not discourage the gutsy flower from the project of giving birth to a new life.

The green buds emerged like miraculous in what became like the survival of the fetus. The desert flower was energized by the heavens that rewarded her efforts in spite of the travails of labouring. Eventually, the great desert flower delivered some aweinspiring corolla with bright petals dancing in the wind and never to be overruled by adversity.

Section Six: Forging Ahead

When the desert flower Mponeng foregrounds the heavens as the source of the much needed rain, she has made an irreversible commitment to forge ahead unmindful of the chaotic circumstances in which she finds herself. Knowing very well that the fury of the adverse conditions is always unrelenting, she makes a further commitment to the organizing principles which are intended to eliminate the chaos that befalls her path. This is a transcendental move that will surely reward her when the rain does fall. In this way, these organizing principles buttress her gutsy and unruffled spirit to enhance her survival experience in the face of extreme conditions.

Risk-Taking Acceptance

To accept the risk
To be gracious hereafter
To acknowledge adversity
To make peace like necessity
Risk taking is acceptable
The risk-taking acceptance

To agitate for acceptance
To adjourn usual resistance
To inculcate the enterprised
Despite speculative despised
To master the syntactic
Hereafter like didactic

CONTEXTUAL COMMENTARY

When the desert flower showed her green buds above ground upon the first rains, it was a risky undertaking. The downpour in the coming days was not properly prepared for. She absorbed some punishment from the falling rain but was accordingly rewarded for braving the elements. She has since bloomed like never before while other desert plants remained underground wondering about the right time to emerge. These desert plants became the late bloomers while Mponeng gained a lot of ground to show off her green and the spotless colours of her petals.

Mponeng understood and appreciated risk as a necessary part of robust existence. Speculative risk separated her from the others. She was willing to take risks in order reap more rewards. While others lagged behind in order to minimize risk, the desert flower Mponeng accepted risk as a platform to maximize returns for which she was handsomely remunerated.

The Desert Dust

The glowing desert dust
Like the heaven's stardust
The dust particles
With mineral dust
Vibrate like energized
To saltate before takeoff
Energized by convection

Convection relays the topsoil
To great distances of the earth
Across the great oceans
They transport the microbial
Far afield like convivial
The distant rain lactates
To breastfeed the desert
Forever thankful for the rainfall

Contextual Commentary

The gentle breeze blows across the desert. The clouds gather across the great sky. The blue sky hides from view. The gentle breeze gains strength as a harbinger of the coming rain. A few drops of rain, like a distant spit of the great Masumu, fall on the dry ground. Sand particles dance in the concomitant mist covered in dust that rises like a sacred incense in grateful tribute to the falling rain. The aroma of the mix of dust and rain titillates the anxious senses of the desert flower. The desert flower gets over-excited over the prospects of the falling rain. Her roots, though cautious, relish the ambient aroma of the falling rain. Unable to wait any longer, Mponeng bursts out of the ground at the first indication of the falling rain.

The Foretaste of Wetting The Shoots

A foretaste of the first rain
Excitement unable to subdue
To relish the falling rain
Despite risks of the floodplain
Entrained to the rainfall
Like a miracle of the lifetime
Here I come good rain
To be gracious I remain

As the flower shoots
The ground breaks open
To allow the sprouts to rise
To blossom before the rain
To welcome the coming rain
The flower springs to life
Like assisted by midwife

CONTEXTUAL COMMENTARY

She seeks the foretaste of wetting her feet even though she is still a greenhorn that is totally unprepared for the torrent of the rainfall, the lashing by the vociferous winds or the crushing by the dust particles. The good rain must come down hard as per the instructions of the heavens even though the baby flower may be overwhelmed by it.

Any collateral damage is the cost of venturing too early and yet there are no regrets on the part of the flower. Any personal damage is a small price to pay for what is now the greatest experience of a lifetime.

Carried On Wings of the Wind

The dry seed of the corolla
Her ruddy beauty like Angola
To depart from here
To venture into the unknown
The future must replenish
To cohere like clannish

When wind speed regains
Wind currents like transport
To carry like convective
The particle adaptive
The momentum like thunderbolt
To arrive before nightfall
To arrive even though unplanned

Contextual Commentary

The great desert flower Mponeng was carried away with a lightning speed on wings of the wind to a new home far from here. In keeping with the way of the Kalahari, she made no demands upon the wind. She did not even question the wisdom or direction thereof. She trusted the wind without reservations for she knew that the boisterous wind was a roaring transport determined to ensure her safe passage. The time-tested wind arrived and became transfixed near the red dunes. The wind cautiously circled around the dunes like a twister for a certain length of time before landing Mponeng on a piece of ground. Mponeng was lodged on hot sand that became her own piece of ground. Now the desert flower could call this piece of ground her own. In this way, she became the master of her own destiny. It's here that she will remain underground until the glorious appearing of the falling rain. Satisfied that Mponeng had attained her own piece of ground, the whirlwind departed in a northeasterly direction into the great expanse of the indomitable Kalahari.

The Crossing To The Other Side

Zebras drill for the voyage
To cross to the other side
Assembled babies must drill
To ditch dry seasons that kill
She teaches them
To remain within view
To transcend the coming surge
If they obey they shall live
To inherit the other side
To venerate the land of the ancestors
Humans averse to risk taking
Because they fear the other side

To disembark a raging flow
Despite hit by waves like a blow
To embrace the unknown
To cross the finish line
Where sorcerers await
To spook the finish line
To impose an incline
The colossal crocodiles lie in ambush
To destroy those easy to fleece
Yet a diligent zebra's kick is fierce
To crush ambushing jaws to fragments
Never more to be victimized by the ambush
Unperturbed by those bewitching the mind

CONTEXTUAL COMMENTARY

The teachings of the African zebra exist forever. These teachings are held to be true in perpetuity. Her unconquerable spirit powers the imagination of many generations on a long and arduous road in the quest to reach their destination where the land is teeming with diversity of vibrant life. As a teacher and professor emeritus, the grandmother zebra has gathered the young to instruct them about the myths and legends of those who have gone before them.

The vicarious stallion and great protector who protects the clan with his life, provides assistance by offering his domain knowledge on the rudiments of tactical defense and survival. The zebra society uses cultural knowledge as a time-tested template on which their survival depends. This gives the young members of society a head start in exploring their natural environment while obeying the supreme law of self-preservation. The green pastures are inviting and the zebras who find them irresistible embark on a journey that requires tenacity to embrace the land that nurtures their way of life.

Vicarious Existence

To ruffle the clan formation
To infuse them with trepidation
A peaceful paradise in disarray
A gallant flesh hereafter affray
To attack them without provocation
To make them flee in their land

Foreign occupation; the chains!
Their motherland is arrested
The tree of defence is parched
The tree nurturing now starched
In this way the tree atrophies
Yet to rise like a furious tree
To honour the land like the Cree
To interject the crushing jaws
Despite arrested by the paws
To live vicariously
To defend furiously

CONTEXTUAL COMMENTARY:

The African zebra assumes the role of a rear guard when the cruel winds of death blow strongly against the clan. The ruthless predators, who throw the clan in disarray, have the power to instill great fear in the hearts of the beautiful zebras. The illustrious stallion with a command of the hardest kick in the African grasslands purposely slows down in order to shield the clan from the cruel blows of death by asphyxiation and simultaneous tearing of the flesh and crushing of the bone. While the zebra does not underestimate the magnitude of demise before him, the selfless stallion accepts the challenge with aplomb and immense bravery so that the clan can live to fight another day. The new generation must forever pay tribute and model themselves after the unequivocal zebra that ensures the clan's survival with his own life.

The Teachings of the African Leopard

To execute a quantum leap
Like a lightening thunderbolt
To pounce despite distanced
Like vulture when incensed
Executing an aerial strike
Hereafter blade claws to compress

A daring hunt despite great risks
To flush, track and strike unassisted
Who watches the back of the legend?
Stealth, elusiveness, grace and prowess
All commendable traits of the trade
Yet the clan unavailable for execution
To master the jungle without the clan?

The geometry of rosettes like insignia
To confirm the origins of her kind
Her explosive pounce like legend
That never dies but persists to infinity
The master of jungle rules struggled
Teaching us to rehearse unfangled
The fluid grace of her way of life
Shall forever serve as a reference

CONTEXTUAL COMMENTARY

When the lions execute a hunting expedition, the clan members are there to provide tactical support such as the flushers, the flankers, the chasers and the striker. When the fearless hyenas face off with domineering lions to reclaim lost ground under the perpetual legend of a hyena queen Phiri Ya Manka, the lions must retreat because they can't repulse the tidal wave of a determined hyena clan led by a formidable queen.

The solitary leopard does not have such tactical support of a cooperative clan and yet she must stand her ground. As a lonesome hunter, she must be a risk assessor, intelligence gatherer, flusher and striker. When she crossed paths with a pack of hunting lions, they were determined to inflict stringent punishment upon her for trespassing. She was cornered by deadly paws which forced her to the ground where lerole la dikatse almost chocked her. Using her agile strength and powerful upper body muscles, she catapulted herself to her feet to fend off the deadly blows already being dished out. Her ability to recover from setback saved the day and she lived to narrate the incredible story to her babies. Despite wounded from that encounter, she was still able to hoist a heavy carcass up the tree.

The teachings of the great African leopard are embedded as part of an institutional memory of African Civilization. In the African cosmology and mythology of the Basotho, the leopard is an insignia of doctoral scholarship. When a traditional surgeon known as Ngaka completed her doctoral studies of Bongaka (doctoral profession) she was awarded a leopard skin and given a new scholarly title Seaparankwe meaning the one who wears a leopard skin. Maaparankwe (the doctoral scholars) were usually hired to serve in the African royal courts. There was even a requirement that a king or queen must complete doctoral studies in order to wear a leopard skin.

Seaparankwe among the Basotho is an equivalent of a PhD scholar who wears a gown in a Western society. Another traditional surgeon known as Nkgekge wore several leopard skins because she was a post-doctoral scholar. The scholarship of Bongaka (doctorate) and Bonkgekge (post-doctorate) has been practiced by the Basotho for thousands of years as attested for in the Sesotho language, the profession of Bongaka, oral history and the traditional surgeons who raised this writer. It is noteworthy that the concept of doctor in Europe as a religious teacher began within the Roman Catholic Church in the 14th century long after the Basotho institution of doctoral scholarship. The English concept of conferring doctoral degrees began in the 16th Century long after Bonkgekge were conferring doctoral degrees in the indigenous university colleges of Bongaka.

As a way forward, the new generation must take a page from the African leopard that looks back like the Sankofa bird before leaping forward. By looking back, they learn from the past before facing the machinations of the path lying ahead.

The Transformative Shame

Like beaten down I became
When cornered by enforced shame
The feeling thus far:
Humbled and shamed like a doghouse
Other concomitants comprise
Guilt and dirt like raped
High spirits spruced and sapped
Feeling numb like used
After misplaced by good intentions

To fall prey to self-injury
Like legendary Emery
Under a cloak of good intentions
The outcome thereof untested
The good thereof unproven
Yet to pursue despite unproven
What happened to self-inquiry?
The machinery of decadence
Stifles inquiry like incandescence

Good intent must interrogate
Like inquisition at the gate
Intended good is rejected
If evidence is contested
Hereafter to transform
Like the great Masumu of Matamong

CONTEXTUAL COMMENTARY

The great Masumu of Matamong sheds his aged skin in order to experience a life changing renewal by means of regeneration. The fearsome Masumu slithers, crawls and rubs between rough surfaces of mountain rock in order to force the stubborn skin to fall away so that he can put it behind him and go on with life. The skin has become restrictive in terms of new vision and new growth. Masumu has outgrown the skin and must discard it. While growing since a child, the rigid skin never kept up and the time has come to change that.

While the process of regeneration is most welcome but like the process of giving birth to a new life, it poses a serious threat to his immediate survival. In fact the threat is like triple jeopardy because (1) during skin shedding he is unable to defend himself, (2) the skin makes him vulnerable when confronted by his adversaries as a result of smudging his good vision and (3) the tightness of the skin hampers his agile movement and striking ability. Without an acute eyesight and agile reaction time he is like a sitting duck waiting for tragedy to befall him. Masumu cannot allow this to happen to him. Those watching him can sense his desperation and frustration as he struggles to shake off and leave behind his ill-fated skin of treachery.

The agonizing and sacred ceremony of skin shedding is initiated when he rubs his head against a rough surface in order to clear his eyes from a blurred vision. Embracing a new vision is item one in the agenda of regeneration. As he scratches and pushes, the skin cracks and begins to peel backward. This slow and painful process cannot be rushed and must happen at a snail's pace using small changes under a tree of an African mathematical knowledge. Masumu takes all the time in the world to regenerate. As he regenerates, the agreeable heavens have already cleared the sky and provided him with the gift of a brilliant sunshine that endows warmth and light like the great incandescence. The land of endless sunshine under him provides tactical support so that he can regenerate on solid ground of the celebrated African soil. He needs and deserves the tactical support because in his normal duties he also serves as a guardian of the African shrines.

The skin is removed in whole so that he can re-enter life using a brand new skin. It cannot be done in pieces, as is the case with other organisms. The requirement for rubbing against rough objects makes this moulting process a particularly painful experience. Nonetheless, Masumu has no choice and cannot defer this process any longer but must divest himself of his disused skin however painful.

Other organisms go to an extent of shedding their exoskeletons in order to grow new ones by undergoing the same process of shedding. These old shells are rigid and confine the organism like a straightjacket that refuses to adapt and fails like a parachute in midair. A dynamic organism throws away the comfort of an old skeletal shell in order to experience the spurts of new growth in accordance with ceremonial demands in the land of the ancestors.

The necessary roughness of the rock surface is extremely vital to revitalize the organism in order to achieve greater heights in life albeit a harsh process to go through. As a matter of urgency and at a specific phase in the life of the organism, the organism must seek, find and endure the necessary adversity that forces it to part ways with old skins, shells, structures and habits that prevent new growth. If the organism cannot stomach this undertaking, it will never grow but will remain stunted and eventually be flattened by its erratic environment as a punishment for failing to respond to the natural variability of its surroundings. Thus, the shedding of the old protective shells forces an introspection.

For this reason, shedding is a necessary loss to be experienced in order to usher a state of renewal by means of regeneration. After shedding his aged skin, the great Masumu of Matamong walked away a new man with a new vision ready to tackle the variability of his environment while jealously guarding the sacred shrines of the ancestors.

Dimakatso

To subdue adversity unfeasible
To transcend misfortune unthinkable
Yet to arise to be a great officer
A ceiling formerly unreachable
Despite sexism that prevailed
Like a star with light to emit
A plastic mind able to retrofit
Dimakatso a desirable combatant
For that rank a determined claimant
To command despite risks
To extend the freedom afar
To free them even at treacherous Darfur

Despite humbled by her beginnings
She was able to unbolt stubborn doors
The daring Dimakatso adjusted well
To persistent obstacles that befell
Like unstoppable despite her gender
Despite unkindness to force surrender
To persevere despite the scar
To sparkle yet volcanic tar
The world salutes a warrior female
Even Canada salutes the Colonel

CONTEXTUAL COMMENTARY

When the fearsome Masumu threatens the naïve mongoose, the mongoose must advance some transcendental moves. She must overcome her naivety. She must overcome her socialized thinking. Moreover, she must trust her instincts. It is this kind of radical transcendence that will give her a survival advantage. When a direct attack seems unfeasible, she can begin with a sideways attack in order to drive a wedge between the indomitable Masumu and his comfort zone. It's when he feels uncomfortable, that the mongoose can directly stage a determined attack. Eventually, Masumu must succumb to the gutsy mongoose that has an instinctive grasp of the volatile situation.

Selective Adaptation

The aged mongoose
Suffered under the cobra
He pleaded with the creator
For survival improvements
He was directed to consider
The speed of the cobra
Adaptive mechanisms began
The mechanisms of selective adaptation

The aged mongoose
Outmatched the cobra
In a simulated environment
He pleaded with the creator
For survival improvements
He was directed to consider
The dancing lightening on QwaQwa mountains
The adaptive mechanisms began
The mechanisms of selective adaptation

The aged mongoose
Like a thunderbolt
Overwhelmed the cobra
In a simulated environment
He pleaded with the creator
For survival improvements
He was directed to embrace
Cellular learning rules
He then became a serious contender

With a lightening megavolt
He attacked like a thunderbolt
To bring demise
To a formidable foe
Previous mechanisms were abortive
Hereafter new mechanisms adaptive

Contextual Commentary

In order for a mongoose to defeat the cobra, it needed self-confidence. Self-confidence is a prerequisite for any serious adaptive behaviour. A molecular adaptation that allowed for a mongoose to be naturally resistant to the snake venom was a game changer in bolstering the much-needed confidence to fight and defeat the cobra. Confidence is like an insurance policy that kicks in when disaster strikes.

The Great Seagull

To arise above ground
To transcend earthbound
Others require airspeed
He advances without airspeed
How is that possible?
To lift himself above ground
Using vertical lift
To go beyond gravity

The caterpillar is earthbound
The seagull is heaven-bound
The vulture requires airspeed
The seagull without airspeed
He rises like didactic
Teaching us the syntactic

The heart-warming sun is brilliant
The blue sky cloudless
While the breeze grooms the grass below
The seagull must return to the sky
To gain a new perspective
To enumerate the relations
To analyze the network
To consider the permutations
Helicopter view attained
While self-interest is restrained

CONTEXTUAL COMMENTARY

When lifting himself from the ground, he must do this to gain transcendence. As he flips his powerful wings, he generates the much-needed lift. The airflow around the wings is comprised by low pressure above the wings and high pressure below the wings. The vector forces of the airflow create the forward movement he needs to take off as simulated by the ancient game of Diketo. As the Basotho describe the movement as Hotherekela it is this kind of movement that gives him the vertical lift of Sefofatsepa.

Unruly Winds

To descend like resized
Meteoric rise like chastized
The albatross defeats great winds
Yet unruly winds reappear
Like a fresh challenge from the rear
Piercing winds like unassailable
To force retraction of the claws
To regain the sky despite the flaws

Troublesome winds of convolution
Like unworthy of revolution
We invoke the heavens
Seeking transcendence
The charging particles power the wings
To climb unruly winds like stepping stones
To gracefully adorn the sky
To refuse defeats that vilify
Great albatross reclimb the wind
To recharge wings however skinned

CONTEXTUAL COMMENTARY

When the powerful winds blew against the rough cliff in the surging blue sea, the resulting turbulence created an updraft. The albatross dived into the wind currents that propelled him into the great sky. He navigated the various wind currents to lock into the one that propelled him forward into greater heights. Eventually, he reached a cruising altitude not having exhausted his energy reserves. His economy of flight and navigational prowess provided an energy source of powerful flight. We shall forever pay tribute to the great albatross with powerful wings. He takes to the great and turbulent skies without fear using a fraction of his flight energy to subdue and climb the high speed winds that can clock more than 800 kilometers per hour.

Section Seven: The Struggle

To survive under barren conditions, necessitates an audacious and serene acceptance with respect to a transcendental sense of sacrosanct purpose to transmute the raw materials of adversity into an electric energy that recharges the spiritual batteries like a battery charger. This instinctive grasp of the higher purpose has philosophical implications so that it is no longer necessary to be morose under prohibitive conditions. Moreover, it is seemingly possible to break the hard shell of impossibility in the same way that a small mongoose defeats an overpowering cobra despite its killer venom. Resonance, like a synergy of the higher purpose and the sense of urgency, lubricates a pipeline of transcendental moves to output more potent energy so that the organism can vibrate as it was intended to vibrate in accordance with the sophisticated purpose of the organizing principles.

Venturesome Kisses

On the narrow path we converged
Heart-warming kisses we exchanged
Blanketed by the African nightfall
In the bushy trees near the Kalahari
Every kiss a sweet windfall safari

Into the night under the stellar universe
We traded hugs to a heart's content
Stars blinked at lovers' romance
Creaking insects melodious dance
The adventure of forbidden kisses
Surpassed all perils that awaited us
The forbidden kisses were true
Each kiss sweetened by the African dew

Like a dew wetting the tulips
Mouth-watering kisses grazed the lips
A sweet kiss in the killer jungle
Tasted sweeter than life itself
Life-extending kisses in the bush
Were ended too soon by ambush

The kisses were punctuated
with indelible blood
when the umbilical cord
snapped between brutal scissors
by perils belying the path
on forbidden grounds

Now beyond the great Atlantic
The heart still crying
for a fugitive of Keetmanshoop
As though I am still hooked
on the memory of the past
this hook is tearing me
Like a fish in a hook of its own

CONTEXTUAL COMMENTARY

Forbidden grounds of love cast their spell. The naivety of love sweetens the love that exists like a desert flower[32]. Deprived of water, the flower waits underground until, when the rains fall, it springs to life, knowing that the rain will soon be gone.

---

[32] This poem *Venturesome Kisses* has inspired the writing of this book The Sacred Knowledge of the Desert. This poem was written in the jungles of Northern Botswana in the Dukwe Refugee Camp in 1988. A Nama lady of Keetmanshoop is the inspirational source of the contextual poem. The Nama people, together with other African natives, created the Afrikaans language in the 1700s while working in the Dutch settlements in the Cape Colony. This poem is a tribute to a great people of Southern Africa.

In the Belly of the Beast

In the belly of the beast
Emancipating change ceased
Ingested, soon to be deceased
When hydrochloric flow
Exacts a cruel blow
The squeezing is aggressive
Despite accommodative
The wounded vegetative

Souls broken by the digestive
Embedded like vindictive
In the belly of the beast
Resistance is futile
Hereafter to exit the digestive
A shift of strategic direction
To emancipate the ingested
To avoid becoming digested

A conniving beast is mouthful
Unquestioning soul is hopeful
The first line of defence
To regain the distance
To reject the ingestion
To evade irresistible digestive
To empower the mind like instinctive

CONTEXTUAL COMMENTARY

The great waterfalls of Hog's Back in the Canadian City of Ottawa broke upon the dark chocolate rocks in the backdrop of the brilliant sun. As the beautiful sun added more luminance, my camera rolled to capture the picturesque moments.

Across the raging waterfalls, a tall bird stood motionless on a black rock like a sentinel on shallow water. Armed with a powerful beak, the bird was oblivious to my presence while she lay in ambush for a gullible fish.

An unwary fish swam by to inspect the ground when the swift bird struck like a lightening flash. After swallowing the fish whole, the bird resumed a motionless position as if nothing had happened while the fish kicked and undulated inside its stomach. The resistive gyrations of the fish were observable and thought provoking at a distance. Unable to help the fish as a result of the violent rapids which threatened to gobble me up, I stood in awe knowing that the digestive juices were already at work to subdue the fish.

Despite a good faith attempt to break free from inside the bird, as confirmed by hard kicks, the effort was futile in facilitating a swift exit from the belly. Even though the fish may have developed a warm and fuzzy feeling that it was doing everything right to win its freedom, it was all an illusion.

Probably the fish realized at some point that hard kicking was not productive and switched to a peaceful strategy of negotiating a safe passage on compassionate grounds but the insatiable bird's position was to ask for a moratorium on militant resistance by the fish so that the process could run its course unopposed. This seemed like a reasonable consideration except that it put the fish at a survival disadvantage because the fish was negotiating from a position of weakness. Extra time was advantageous to the bird while it sealed a permanent fate of the fish in the belly. The bird favoured more time because it was a matter of time before the digestive juices broke the back of the resisting fish.

When the fish stopped making any movement it was apparent that the digestive juices had managed to asphyxiate the fish. It was impossible to escape from inside the bird without some external help. How can a fish or anyone win an emancipation struggle from the belly of the beast?

Survival Advantage

To traverse while cultureless
To cross like an eagle plumeless
Hereafter in the terrain clueless
To be circumscribed by naivety
To be constrained by some disdain
To walk hitherto without a memory
A tragic blow to the beautiful Emory

In the absence to be dethroned
Disconnected from pre-existence
To defer to some variable circumstance
Unbounded by the problem space
Unable to see the subspace
The formidable overrules like ballistic
Unable to conjugate the syntactic

The struggle raging is not new
Perpetual encoding is before us
Encoded knowledge is instructive
The deciphering like addictive
To entice the subspace engaged
Unruly fangs hereafter assuaged
Survival advantage our directive

CONTEXTUAL COMMENTARY

The dynamic environment presents new-fangled challenges to the organism which must respond in novel ways in order to gain a survival advantage. From time to time Mother Nature exacts harsh punishment upon an organism which is not flawlessly drilled for the challenges lying ahead.

The young African eagle, instructed by the great mother eagle, continuously spreads and beats its wings with occasional short flights in the simulated environment of the mother nest in brave anticipation of that eventual maiden flight. Interestingly, the mother nest is a source of cultural knowledge which provides a template of time tested solutions to the environment that experiences a constant state of perturbation.

To respond correctly to the volatility of the punishing environment, the organism must preferably be capable of extremely fast paced learning. Sometimes this is not possible given a short space of time with respect to the required efficacy whereby a margin of error would trigger a sudden demise of the organism. In this special case the organism must alternately rely on pre-knowledge of its cultural heritage that is well suited to the gyrations of the environment. This kind of cultural knowledge shortens the learning curve and fills in the blanks without which the organism is guideless. The distilled knowledge of culture provides the critical survival tools that allow the organism to tackle everything that gets thrown its path. In this way, the effervescent young eagle is a rehearsed practitioner of novel and robust techniques in grateful tribute to the memory of its origins.

Survival Analytics

Survival analytics
Mental therapeutics
To understand what's going down
To reclaim lost grounds
To lay claim like never before
To make amends with the past
In the land of the ancestors

A meticulous attention
A decisive precondition
Instinctive grasp of infinitesimal
The directive to avert the abysmal
Conveying much respect to the stochastic
A graceful acceptance despite ballistic
Without some events that inspire
We proceed like unbroken sapphire
To agitate for change that refuses to yield
To concentrate efforts that vindicate
Agitation cleanses the soul
To purify towards a goal

CONTEXTUAL COMMENTARY

Previous memories of defeat in the deadly embrace were not enough to deter the new generation of the mongoose from engaging in the analysis of the slick movements of the fearsome cobra. Although many would find it too painful to absorb the stomach-turning accounts of defeat, the mongoose detached herself from the mortality of pain in order to begin a paradigm shift in the new struggle to defeat a previously powerful opponent.

The goal of the African mongoose was to stake her claim to the rare fruits of a hard won victory resembling the unconquerable queens of Nubia like Queen Candace who caused Alexander the Great to freeze and retreat when the Nubian armies stood up to him. A painstaking reflection revealed that it was possible to overrun the cobra in a gutsy move by delivering the first decisive blow like a thunderbolt.

Endless days of rehearsing had perfected her interpretive and combative skills and thus produced the indomitable African mongoose. Attention to detail ensured a short but decisive victory against a slithering foe capable of reinventing the art of war. A new dispensation had irrevocably arrived when the mongoose became a newly crowned ruler of the shifting ground despite the cobra having a reach advantage in a treacherous terrain. Photographic memory bolstered her survival advantage because by memorizing the repertoire of an aweinspiring cobra, she had garnered enough depth and breadth to become the architect of her own destiny.

Dichotomous Existence

To stick to the ground like glue
To embrace hereafter to subdue
To subdue the dichotomous
To vandalize the thalamus
Hereafter dichotomous existence

To disown like illegitimate gain
To scar the innocent membrane
Cellular bond weakening
From itself partitioning
Cracked by acoustic thunder
Forced hitherto asunder
Hereafter dichotomous existence

To contain using the forensic
To diminish using the agnostic
To dematerialize survival
To disjoint trust that belongs
Gentle restraint invisible adhesive
Embraced hereafter oppressive
Hurtful membrane of the thalamus
Hereafter forever dichotomous

CONTEXTUAL COMMENTARY

Discriminatory avoidance learning is the most stressful experience on the plasticity of the cellular membrane of the brain cells of the organism. It disrupts memory formation and pulls the equilibrium away from tranquility and rationality. The Canadian society of Ottawa subjects some members of her population to this form of extreme stressful experience. The gentle oppression, as practiced by the great society of Ottawa, has inculcated a permanent sense of dichotomy in the minds of the socioeconomically disenfranchised communities forcing them to forever struggle with a painful legacy of identity crisis. Like the disenfranchised children of the beautiful cuckoo, the members of these communities are forever reminded that they do not belong.

The Missing Platform

The basis was not there
The platform was missing
The stepping-stones far apart
Unable to navigate
They refused the reciprocal
Preconditions equivocal
As if undeserving to be here
The missing platform enforced

Events required transcendence
To transcend social conditioning
Sense impressions adapting
Radical transcendence enforced
To transcend without examples
To exceed properties of the object
Polished like a diamond
Despite trusting beyond

CONTEXTUAL COMMENTARY

The successful adaptation of the organism is not possible when directionless. The organism must be characterized by goal orientation and single purpose in order to be directed in the majority of the times.

When the great seagull flaps its powerful wings using the upstroke and the downstroke, there is a momentary wobbling of its body as the feet lift off and then touch off the ground like a beginner. The apparent inelegance is an elaborate deception of its great flight mastery. For this reason, the apparent inelegance serves the function of keeping the bird humble when approaching the heavens.

The thrust of the efforts of the bird pulls it in the right direction of flight and eventually the bird takes off as if effortlessly in the right direction of the heavens. The wings of the seagull are powered by consistent faith in its ability to execute a successful flying maneuver. The bird understands that life exacts harsh punishment upon a directionless flight that is not well rehearsed for takeoff.

Emancipating Pedagogues

To converge hitherto
To consult at Potchefstroom
To architect solutions via SELEN
Solution framework for the fallen
To deliberate, they must congregate
To emancipate, they must conjugate
To solve the problem domain
To emancipate despite the pain

The great son of Mahlomaholo
Has assembled the great minds
A phenomenal exercise assembled
When the gutsy, grill the exercise
The melting pot, must contextualise
Never more to be circumscribed
Like a maiden flight, undefined!
To interrogate like synaptic
To articulate the syntactic

Contextual Commentary

A buffalo parent who cares about the survival of her young buffalo in the African grasslands may find it reasonable that learning the ways of the predatory lions would confer a survival advantage to the young buffalo at which point she commits the young buffalo to the lion school. The subjects of study require clawing, swiping, stealth walking, stalking, tearing and puncturing flesh using the canines including the most difficult maneuver of tree climbing which the lions themselves haven't been able to master. The school utilizes claws, paws, and canines as material objects of learning.

As time progresses, the previously enthused buffalo begins to slow down after finding it difficult to process the teachings of the lion. Despite the young buffalo raising a number of pertinent questions about the teaching and learning situation, the lion school authorities do not incorporate the buffalo methods of natural defence like stomping, charging, goring and ground assault. In fact the lion teachers pejoratively discount the use of stomping or horns as lacking in evolutionary sophistication citing the feline ability to open and retract the claws, while in motion, as the only skills worthy of accreditation in the University of the African Jungle.

Unable to relate to the teachings, the young buffalo begins to drift on account of a dichotomous existence. It gets even harder to embrace the buffalo community because the new experience has become a wedge between the young buffalo and other buffalos. What will it take to engineer a more relevant form of teaching and learning which relates and re-awakens the prowess of the buffalo as the indomitable ruler in the African grasslands?

Emotional Numbness

He or she is remote
Unable to emote
To fall short like asymptote
To fail to touch the asymptote
Facial expression robotic
Like unexploded ballistic
Cerebral mastery of syntactic
Mechanically wired robotic
Emotional numbness
Emotional absence

To explode like the ballistic
To disregard the syntactic
Unable to emote is ruthless
Like ballistic is emotionless
Incapable of empathy
Unable to connect emotionally
Unwired at the Eukaryotic
Unable despite Eucharistic
Emotionally numb
Emotionally absent

CONTEXTUAL COMMENTARY

The brain structure PLT is responsible for emotional processing. It can be induced, through environmental conditioning, to become fear based and over-reactive to an environmental stimulus. If another brain structure PFC does not balance out the PLT then an organism is a cold fish with no altruistic sentiments. Such a cold-blooded organism becomes a threat to the survival of those who stray into its life's orbit.

A Guarded Experience

Peeled to the core like onion
Unhitched like chain from union
To walk the path alone
To conceal the struggle scars
To guard them against the agnostic
The taboo cutting the enteric
Abrasive salt burns like sulphuric

The tyranny of the syntactic
Necessitates whiteness of the Arctic
To subdue scars that defy curtailment
Never more to express a dark pain
To subdue like aggressive
To entice like abrasive
To instill oppressive feeling
To avoid blemishing the Arctic
To remain guarded like ballistic

How long to remain guarded?
To confine to praise singing?
While the internals are rumbling?
Prohibition via the syntactic
With inferred support by the agnostic
May explode like instinctive
To cleanse them like corrective

CONTEXTUAL COMMENTARY

The grandmother mongoose drills the young for the do-or-die mission that awaits them. The time is right for the young to learn from the indefatigable huntress about the slippery ways of the breath-taking Masumu of Matamong. The great Masumu inspires awe when lifting his puffed hood above ground so as to assume a domineering posture at all times.

The grandmother mongoose has defeated Masumu many times and seeks to exorcise the impressionable young of the aweinspiring spell that Masumu may cast upon them. She excites the young about the great exploits of the legendary hunters who captured Masumu using novel ways which Masumu did not anticipate.

The granny urges the neophytes to take a page from the cultural knowledge of the ancients in order to gain a survival advantage over Masumu and fend off his hypnotic and crafty ways. The full moon in the new year of Phato in the Sesotho calendar brightened the path as the young initiates listened intently to the selfless matriarch of the clan. The unconquerable queen, made stronger by adversity, commands an institutional memory which the young must embrace in order to replenish the fountain of knowledge on behalf of those coming after them and thus better the ways of persistence in a fluid terrain that changes like shifting sand.

A Mindless Existence

To deflate like punctured
To exist like captured
Reluctant to apply the mind
The mind hereafter to unwind
Like a bird with broken wings
Rule adherence is secondary
Abdominal like possessive
A thinking mind like excessive

Below the navel like electric
Then to explode like ballistic
Existence hitherto barbarized
Intelligence hereafter motorized
Unthinking state like bliss
Intelligence like adversarial
A mindless existence
A machine-like existence

CONTEXTUAL COMMENTARY

For an organism to process a novel stimulus, it requires short-term memory, long-term memory and past knowledge hereafter referred to as SLP. The strategic purpose of SLP is to ensure a productive problem solving behaviour in order to gain a survival advantage on behalf of the organism. The utility of SLP assists the organism in gaining transcendence over a problem space by learning from the experience without being over consumed by the new contraptions of the stimulus. The application of SLP necessitates some degree of moral code, mental sharpness and instinctive grasp of the situation to facilitate a real-time processing of the stimulus regardless of its positive or negative conditioning. An SLP capable organism is unruffled by the emotional triggers of the stimulus.

An organism that survives an extreme experience like a headless chicken can still process a novel stimulus but without the SLP survival advantage. This was the case in the great village of Mmakwane in the Free State province of South Africa when the headless chicken, dipped in boiling water, flapped its wings and lashed out its feet in quick successions like a rapid canon fire in a blind attempt to escape. Despite a merciless decapitation, the lower brain structure of the bird, known as medulla oblongata, was still intact making it possible for the bird to carry out the rudiments of life sustenance such as respiration, blood circulation, heartbeat, motor balancing, metabolism and others. However, without the critical functions of SLP such as remembering, analyzing, comparing, modeling, perceiving, creating new synaptic connections and drawing from the knowledge of the past, it was not possible for the headless chicken to resourcefully process all the dimensions and the variability of the stimulus.

A non-SLP organism cannot utilize past experience but must only process the stimulus in the present giving it a primitive one-track approach to the actions of a sensory input as opposed to an erudite organism that uses a multi-track approach to stimulus processing. A typical organism can process a novel stimulus using a literal or symbolic domain and will switch very easily between the two domains. A decapitated organism does not have this enhanced ability of multi-domain processing for the reason that it is only limited to processing the stimulus in a literal domain effectively depriving itself of symbolic processing.

The difference between the literal and symbolic domains is like an analytic difference between arithmetic and algebra. If one only understands arithmetic then one can only work with literal numbers like 1, 2, and 3 as in a literal domain whereas mastering algebra gives you the enhanced ability to process variables like x, y and z as in a symbolic domain. Mastery of both numerical systems endows you with the sophistication of multi-domain switching and processing. Our decapitated organism only understands and responds to literals and relies on a literal understanding of the present stimulus without drawing from the symbolic richness of past knowledge. The survival repertoire of this crude organism can only do fight or flight responses and nothing more.

The Great Lesheleshele

Glutinous like cassava
Volcanic like the lava
To asphyxiate unaware
The bubbles gasping for air
Unlike heated molasses
The bubbles burst like glasses
While stirring the African pot
The legendary Lesokwana
Lesheleshele la nakwana

The bubbles like fuming
Heated fizzes splashing
The outward spiraling
Escaped like trapped lava
Ripped like a shirt to be free
Lesheleshele simmering
Sustained waves like acidic
With periodic sputtering
To repeat like the chevron
To exit the black cauldron

CONTEXTUAL COMMENTARY

When the black beauty of Dipitsa Tse Ntsho became fired up during an evening African fire, their spherical form glowed like a concealed moon of the heavens. Their curved figure was pleasing to behold while spirited flames licked Dipitsa Tse Ntsho as if to groom them. The vivacity of their warm ruddiness like Letsoku was there to ensure that the spirits of Dipitsa Tse Ntsho remained energized by the red hot setting. The great Baile of Matamong looked on with anticipation while the members of the Mlangeni clan remained transfixed in the glow and mysticism of the spherical form.

The sacred task of Hobidisa Hlama Ya Ting and using Dipitsa Tse Ntsho was part of prescribed teachings from the matriarchs of the clan. As a rehearsal teaching, she would ferment Hlama ya Lesheleshele to demonstrate to her eager students a biological enrichment of indigenous foods using natural organic chemistry in accordance with the indigenous teachings from many generations who have gone before them and long before the advent of colonization. The anti-microbial ingredients of Ting have been used to ensure healthy babies and mothers without a need to resort to chemical medicine.

The preservation of this ancient wisdom has since been broken by Afrophobic modernity and it is not apparent if the new generation will take a page from the past to walk in the footsteps of their ancestors. At least for now, the modern generation chooses to suppress the traditions of the past for purposes of appeasing the demands of Eurocentricity and emulating the methods and techniques of modernity. For their own survival, the new generation will have to invoke the legend of Sankofa by taking a page from the past in order to carry on the teachings of the matriarch of the clan.

He Was Like A Bat

He was like a bat
to transcend the ground
unafraid of erratic heights
He got scorched by near death
at lofty cliffs of QwaQwa
He lived in the rock layers
unafraid of serpents ferocious
to take refuge from the heights

He was a misfit
unaccepted by the ground
That feared his transcending ability
they felt he was not one of them
Moreover rejected by the birds
for his wings seemed crude and unfinished
in reality he couldn't freely fly
but could only glide leveraging wind currents
like the great albatross
He needed to latch on to the winds
to lift him into the air
to be lifted from the ground
thus to fly like those that flew
it was this idiosyncrasy
that set him apart from the others

CONTEXTUAL COMMENTARY

The dichotomy of existential struggles proved too painful to master. He was unable to marry the ground and the sky. Unwavering attempts at discriminating among the permutations of the dichotomy left a permanent mark on the membrane of the pyramidal cells; an unintended damage on the plasticity of the membrane.

He thought of approaching the dichotomous conundrum from another angle but he began to hesitate unable to shake off the painful memory of the previous struggles. The setback was so momentous it required adjusting to the shocking anguish. How much time until the nightfall before he makes another move? He may have reached the proximity of a coveted prize but he does not know for sure if this move will not hurt him once more again.

Residual Pieces

The pieces on the ground
Scattering never to be around
To organize the reassembly
To reattach busted pieces
like a forgotten trove
shriveled pieces whiffed like a clove
To reassemble before scattering
To rebuild before nightfall
The residual pieces that disappear

The inexorable scattering
Made it hard for reassembly
To recover after years gone too long
To reattach pieces no more there
To reawaken voices now muted
To catch a distant cloud
To pursue what is no longer there

CONTEXTUAL COMMENTARY

When Manneheng died while the author took refuge underground from the apartheid forces, it dealt a crushing blow to the future efforts of reacquainting the author with his roots.

One regrettable fact is that maybe the little African boy should have defied tradition to find out more about his roots before nightfall. Little did he know that someday he would have to contend with looking at a graveyard without being able to invoke the voices now deeply buried underground.

The Atlantic

The cold body of water
A great divide from afar
Winds begin to get rough
The waves rise to engulf
To affront them with antithesis
To make them drift from their genesis
Hereafter the great Atlantic
Forever overruled by syntactic

Distance imposed with coldness
To punish them for boldness
Unmindful of humble beginnings
Love left behind to atrophy
Even new love to be punished
Hereafter resolved to fight the Atlantic
Never more overruled by the syntactic

CONTEXTUAL COMMENTARY

From time to time the great expanse of the Atlantic ocean becomes an impassable divide between the beginnings of the landings of an individual in a new country. The euphoric energy that originally fired the individual fades away and the individual is only forced to deal with the cold nuts and bolts of architecting a new beginning in the new land.

The antithesis that comes in a form of pejorative characterizations of his person and the syntactic demands of culture shock becomes a permanent fixture. Can a defenseless and uprooted individual take on the Atlantic in order correct the injustices which are hard like a jagged rock but invisible like a smooth glass?

The Finish Line

To succeed the marathon
To overreach oblivion
We want to embrace you
To bask under your glare
Great athletes burst forth
To outdistance the baseline
To arrest the finish line

The desirable treacherous
When converging like sorcerous
To spook the finish line
To slow them down in their tracks
To hesitate near the finish line
Hereafter, to break the jinx
To arrive like a twister
To explode like canister

CONTEXTUAL COMMENTARY

When the cell membrane is polarized at $-70mV$, it requires a strong electrical impulse to break the limits of resistance in order to depolarize. The impulse must have enough energy to move the cell membrane in order to open the ion channels. If the stimulus commands adequate positive energy, it causes the membrane channels to open in order to trigger the chemical reactions within the cytoplasm of the cell. With the intensity of the stimulus being strong enough, a chemical message is dispatched to the nucleus to deploy the RNAs for a special protein synthesis. If the purpose of the protein is memory formation, the assembled protein is electrically sent down the axon to marshal a strong synaptic connection. Hereafter, the memory shall forever be engraved and never to be forgotten.

Is There a Real Me?

To disclaim the inner being
To discount like a slave king
To be like a water source
To be drinkable after filtering
Despite a good faith attempt
Non-conformist to preempt
To deny existence of my core
To diminish real me like a flaw
Is there a real me?
How can there be?

To entrench the real like Achilles' heel
To subdue the innermost to appeal
To diminish interest in emery
To get hitched to an alien memory
To accept the unacceptable
To believe the unbelievable
To agitate, beautifully unfazed
To restrain, punitively unpraised
Are they for real?
Is there a real me?

CONTEXTUAL COMMENTARY

A filtered existence in the beautiful society of Ottawa has caused the passage of time to slip unnoticed. The great society says "to be real" and yet unaccepting of the real me. What kind of "real me" are they looking for? I have presented the appeasing self and they embraced me like never before thus inviting me to the dinner tables. I presented my African "real me" and they rebuffed me like never before never to invite to the dinner tables. Shocked and awed, I was dazed while the years ticked past me like a rocket train of Toronto's subway. Eighteen years later I still don't know my "real me". There is no real me. I am who I am and to be who I am for I must embrace my humble beginnings even when I reach big endings.

Scripted Existence

We must fulfill a script
We must execute the program
The lady at Live Bridge
Insisted on a scripted response
She allowed no room for departure
We were graded on a scripted response

I want to stray from the script
To enhance without the script
I can do a superb work this way
But I become penalized
For venturing outside the script
Like a dead body lying in crypt
On account of the extreme cold
On the ground ready to scold
I feel arrested by the script
I must break free from the mould
So that I can architect destiny I behold
Never more to lead a scripted existence

CONTEXTUAL COMMENTARY

The great and beautiful society of Ottawa prescribes a scripted existence to her inhabitants. A variety of rules provide guidance to the behaviour. The administrative machinery requires an interaction based on the rules even though you may not have had an input in them by virtue of being a disenfranchised individual. This highly regulated existence impacts all aspects of social life. What then happens to the internal dreams and hopes of those who live outside the rubric of bureaucratic control? Do they atrophy and shrivel away while an individual works hard to serve the bureaucratic machinery which he does not fully understand how it works?

Solving the Present

The eyes strain to see the crescent
The mind retreats from the present
Prohibition of a breastfeeding glow
Will succumb under a subsequent blow
To back away from the crescent
To disengage from the present
To disrelish
To disengage

The mind averse to a stuffed envelope
The neuron retreats like an antelope
To back away to fight another day
To obey the brain in the stomach
A tactical regroup
To uncouple the goop
Trapped like a pheasant
Solving the present

CONTEXTUAL COMMENTARY

The first brain which an organism was fitted with resided in the stomach. The enteric brain was concerned with the immediate survival of the organism.

Supported by a population of one billion neurons, the enteric commands more neurons than the spinal cord and is capable of functioning autonomously even after being severed from the central nervous system. The ability to solve the present depends very much on the prompts of the brain in the stomach and how much an organism is responsive to it.

The Conclusion

The <u>Sacred Knowledge of the Desert</u> demonstrates an African origin of philosophical thought and how this came about as a result of the African natives tracing their genesis to Mokgubu wa Kganare (The Galactic Core). The African philosophy of science, as shown with respect to the African theory of matter, demonstrates an unbreakable link between the cosmos and the African natives. The fluid-based theory of matter underscores the fact that matter is continuous.

The five constructs of Basotho philosophy cast more light and broaden our knowledge frontier in terms of the philosophical principles of *truth, wisdom, analysis, knowledge* and *ethics*. The book shows that logic is a subset of the truth of Koma as opposed to the Western society in which logic is the superset of the truth. The cosmic knowledge exerts great influence on the African natives and their way of life including their mathematical knowledge, architectural tradition, indigenous medicine and their survival strategies which derive efficacy from the cosmos in accordance with the majestic stars of the heavens such the legendary *Selemela, Mphatlalatsane, Sefalabohoho, Tosa, Tosamasiu,* and *Makgakga,* among others.

The different sections of the book such as *Transcending, Self-Preserving, Self-Restraining, Glorious Appearing, Forging Ahead* and *The Struggle* testify to the inherent power of the human spirit to transcend adversity by learning from and emulating the great spirit of the desert flower Mponeng of the indomitable Kalahari.

You are encouraged to read these pages carefully in order to allow their principles to sink in to usher the transformative power of <u>The Sacred Knowledge of the Desert</u>. Take a page from the great bird of the sky as expressed in the contextual poem *The Great Seagull* or *The Missing Platform*. Despite his ability to perform a flawless execution using vertical lift, sometimes the great seagull wobbles as if he is a beginner but this apparent inelegance is an elaborate cover of his great mastery of flight. It is as if he approaches the heavens with utmost humility. A selfless behaviour of this kind from the great master of flight is a sacred template that we must emulate in order to become better humans.

Books

The Sacred Knowledge of the Desert	*ISBN: 978-0-620-59937-5*
African Origin of Mathematics	*ISBN: 978-0-620-64428-0*
A Woman in the Bush	*ISBN: 978-0-620-52381-3*
A Goodbye To My Little Troubles	*ISBN: 978-0-9730744-0-6*
Sesotho Dictionary of Mathematics	*ISBN: 978-0-620-51031-8*
Songs of Hope (chapter)	*ISBN: 978-0-973-36926-7*
The Color Medicine	*Unpublished M.S.S*
Ontological States of the Object	*Unpublished M.S.S*
The Philosophy of the Triangle	*Unpublished M.S.S*
Indigenous Mathematical Concepts	*Unpublished M.S.S*
The Heart of Our Community (chapter)	*ISBN: 0-9733692-8-0*
The Sangoma and the Microscope	*ISBN: 978-0-620-58783-9*

Scholarly Papers and Articles

1. *The African Origin of Mathematics*, The Thinker: Pan African Quarterly Journal, Johannesburg, South Africa, 2014.
2. *African Origin of Mathematical Teaching and Learning*, Proceedings of the 40th Annual International Conference of the Southern African Society for Education, North West University, Mafikeng, 26-28 September 2013.
3. *African Telegraphy and Indigenous Innovation*, Southern African Society for Education, North West University, Mafikeng, South Africa, 2013.
4. *The Formidable Crossing*, Africa Unbound, United Nations Economic Commission for Africa, Addis Ababa, Ethiopia, 2011.
5. *The Triangle: A Tool of Analysis*, The Thinker Vol. 21, Vusizwe Media, South Africa, 2010.
6. *Historicity of Realtime Chronicles*, The Thinker Vol. 19, Vusizwe Media, South Africa, 2010.
7. *The Organic Roots of the African Matrilineal Society*, Africa Unbound Magazine, 2010.
8. *Design Theory of Letanta*, African Journal of Science, Technology, Innovation and Development, UK, 2009.
9. *Removable Discontinuity*, Sheila Copps Meets African Caribbeans, St Paul University, Ottawa, Canada 2004.
10. *Where Are You Lady?* in Kola, McGill University, Montreal, Quebec, Canada, 1993.
11. *Freedom Fighters and Spirit Mediums*, Carleton University, Ottawa, Canada, 1993.

12. *Brief Notes on Thekwini*, Safra, Ottawa, Canada.
13. *History of Makholokoe – Part I*, Zulumathabo on the Internet.
14. *History of Makholokoe – Part II*, Zulumathabo on the Internet.

Figure 7 *South African Moon*

Figure 8 *Diketo system*

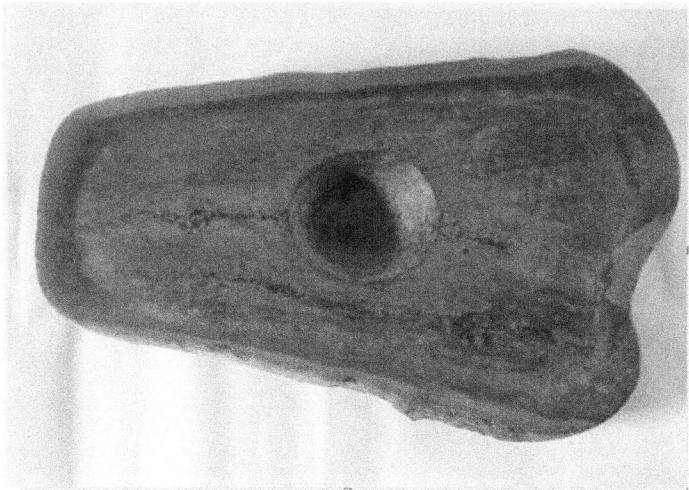

Figure 9 *The author and the son in Canada's bitter cold*

Figure 10 *Ditema writing system*

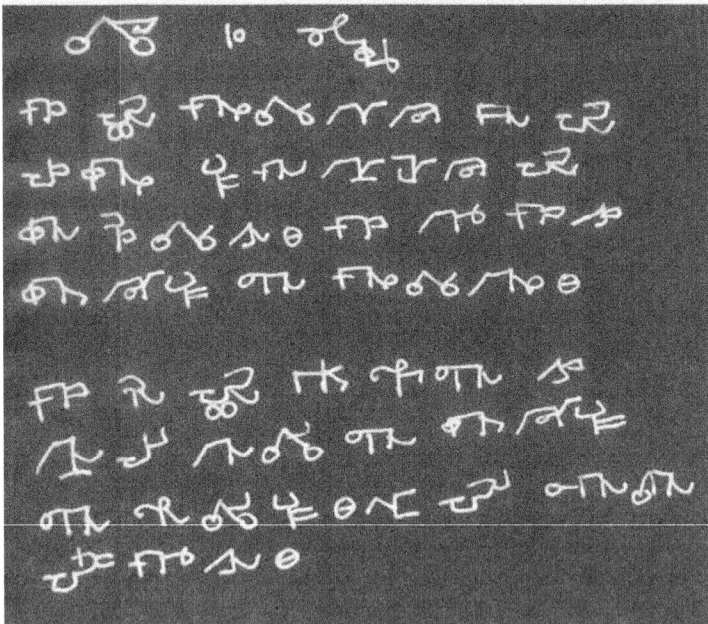

Figure 11 *Ditema glyphs for Matamong ceremony*

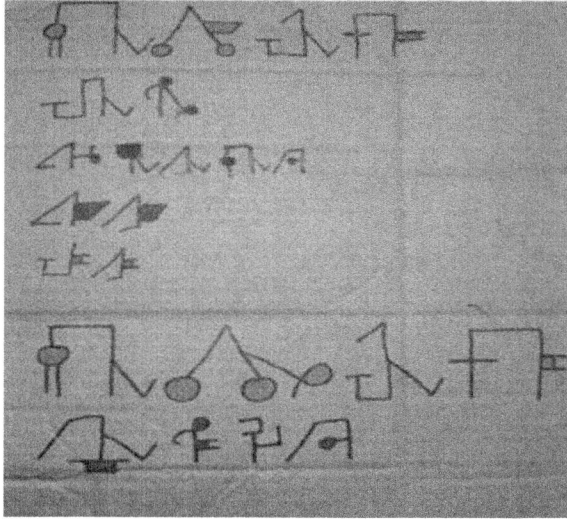

Figure 12 *Triangle showing three problem causations*

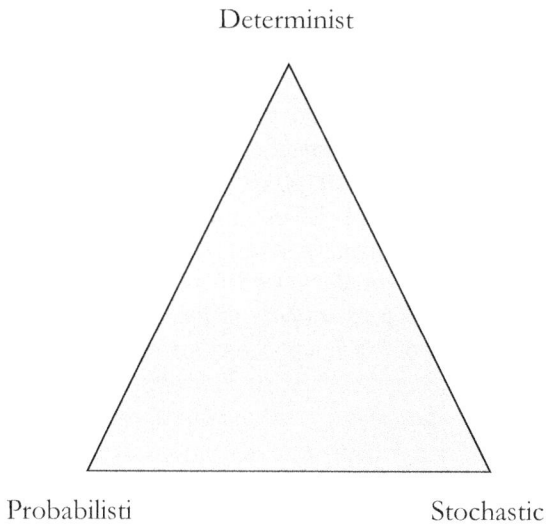

Determinist

Probabilisti

Stochastic

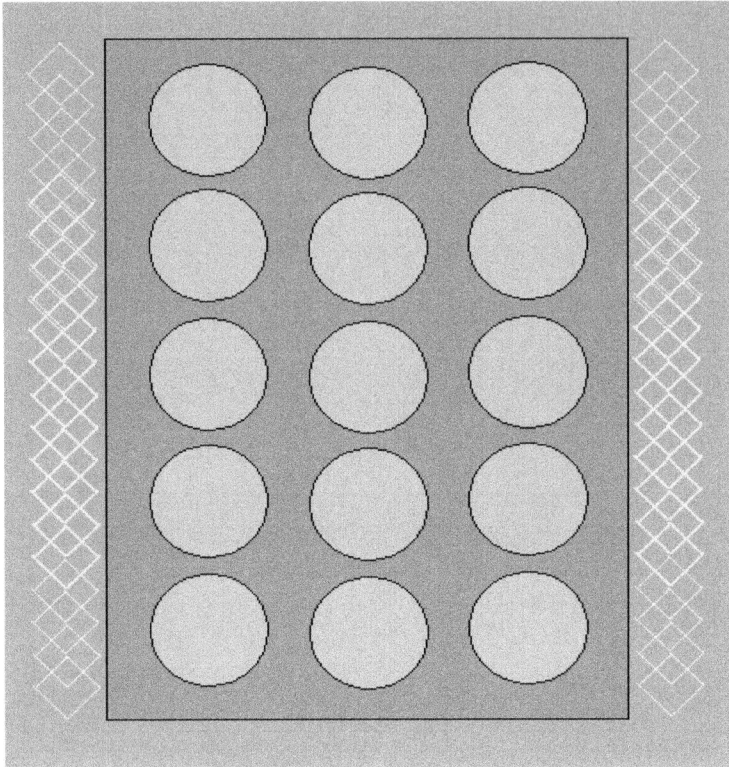

Moruba is a numerical calculator with a built-in gaming console. It has the capability of five mathematical operations namely (1) addition, (2) subtraction, (3) multiplication, (4) division and (5) concatenation. At the time when Europe was without a fully functional mechanical calculator, the African mathematicians and engineers of the Kingdom of Mapungubwe in Southern Africa used this computational device to compute and perform record keeping of their transactions. These transactions were part of the Indian ocean mercantile system which included countries such as South Africa, Zimbabwe, Malawi, Zambia, Botswana, Mozambique, Kilwa and numerous other East African nations. The goods and services sold reached far away nations such as Turkey, India, China and others. Such was the commercial sophistication of African civilization in Southern Africa long before the advent of Euro-Christian colonization.

Left to Right: Software Engineers: Iranian colleague and the author at a Google's company Adscapemedia in Ottawa, Canada. Both were among the company's team members who were flown to San Francisco to demonstrate newly engineered software to the executives and software

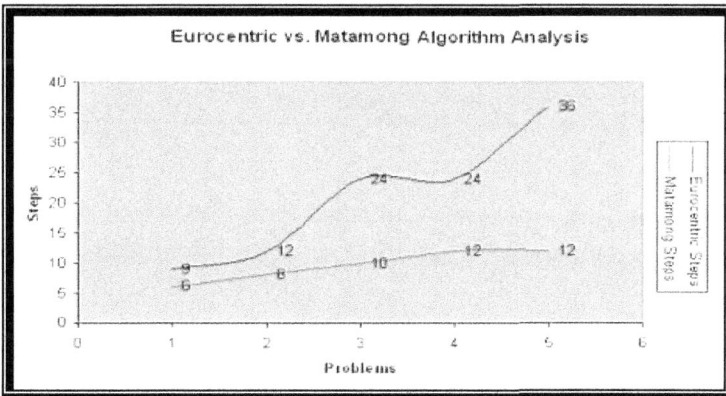

Analytic double graph showing an African mathematical algorithm (logarithmic line) showing less sensitivity to a problem input size as opposed to a Eurocentric method (polynomial line) which grows fast in response to an input size. The implication is that the most efficient algorithm is the one that demonstrates a logarithmic behaviour.

141